SECURING THE C LEVEL

Getting, Keeping, or Reclaiming that Executive Title

MICHAEL D. PETERS

Copyright © 2012 Michael D. Peters
All rights reserved.

ISBN: 146796882X
ISBN-13: 9781467968829

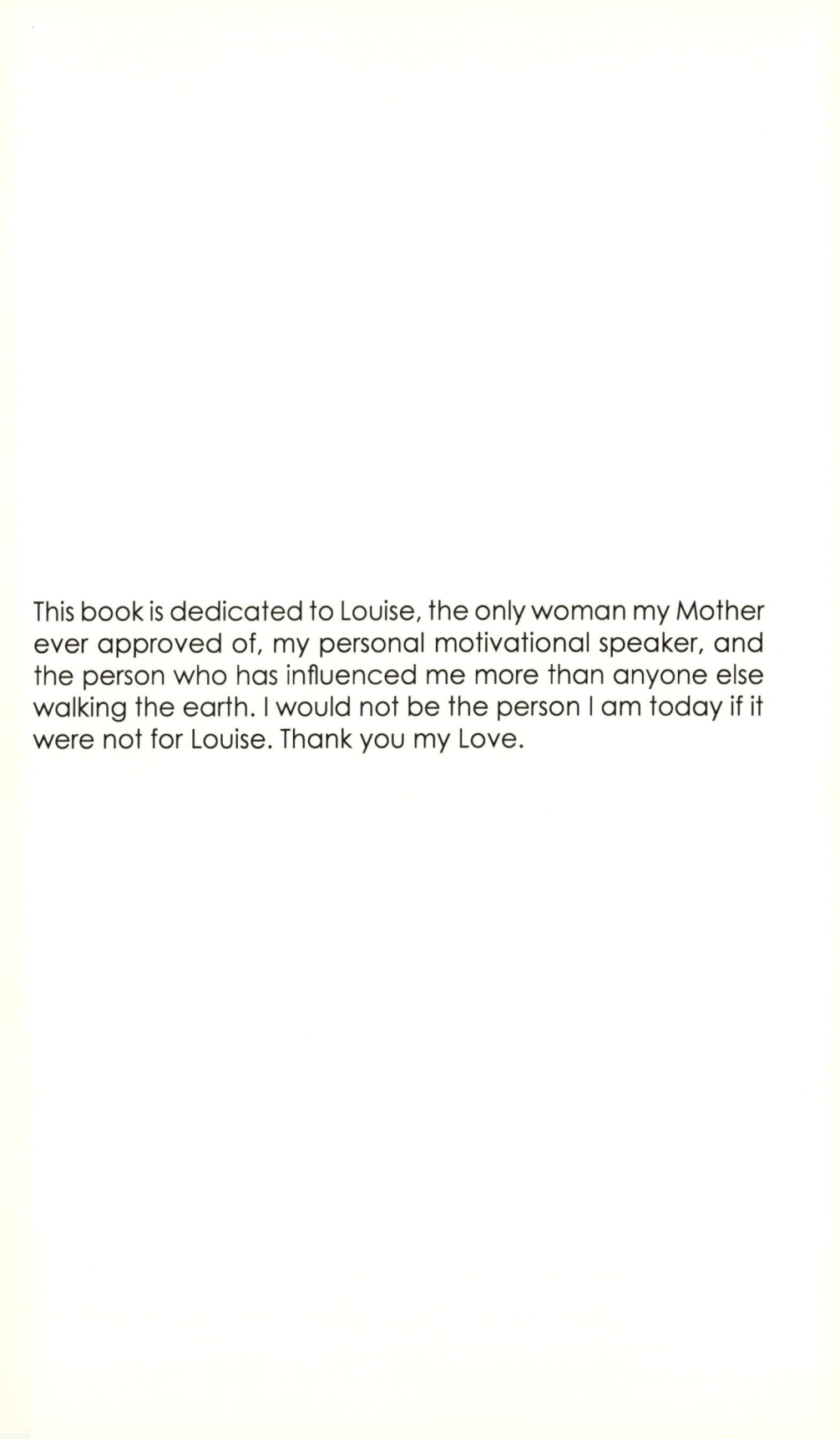

This book is dedicated to Louise, the only woman my Mother ever approved of, my personal motivational speaker, and the person who has influenced me more than anyone else walking the earth. I would not be the person I am today if it were not for Louise. Thank you my Love.

Preface

For as long as there are leadership positions available, there will be leadership transitions. These changes and the opportunities or challenges they pose to ambitious leaders are as ancient as human civilization. Leadership challenges have not become less complex as society advances but in reality have become more complex because of all of the new and emerging business drivers that directly affect how business gets conducted. This change that affects the corporate leadership ranks may seem overwhelming, but rejoice! You are not alone. Others have successfully or unsuccessfully gone before you and they will serve you well.

This book is your roadmap for taking charge of your executive career and aspirations. You have the power to create significant positive change in your life. There are really only two choices to make when you approach those crossroads and that is that either you can change You, the "Me, Myself, and I" facet, or you can change It, "The Challenge." The most important thing we can do in life is have a plan. Our plan should be adaptable because that plan will serve as the framework for our success throughout our lives. Don't believe for an instance that your aspirations are not achievable because you would be mistaken. While it may seem that for some people you may know, everything is easy, and virtually handed to them on a silver platter, the reality is that with the appropriate amount of concerted effort and strategic, albeit cunning maneuvers, we have the absolute potential to achieve everything we want as well. You can achieve all things included in what I will refer to as your personal career progression project plan. The challenge is to secure that executive level corporate position fulfilling your aspirations and ambitions, right?

For many years, I have examined the challenges facing executives and, at the same time, I have climbed the corporate ladder. If you are reading this book, it is no doubt because you either aspire to join the elite executive ranks, or you are interested in maintaining your lofty position, or lastly, you have suffered a set-back and want to come back with vigor. The first big section of this book will focus on getting to the point of securing that executive leadership position where we will explore strategic plans, goals structuring, credential building, and sequencing of events and execution. The second part of this book examines the how to keep your executive position within a corporation and we will explore corporate culture, leadership style, competitive hazards, political relationships, and opportunities that will help you keep your executive position. Finally, the remaining portion of this book will examine the reclaiming component that frequently faces current leaders holding executive positions as they navigate adversity and unfortunate change. We will explore together ways to be more effective during interview negotiations, using covert technology legally, credential building, social networking, and refining your personal marketing spin cycle.

My hope is that this book will assist and inspire you to achieve that executive level objective and equip you with a new set of progressive tools that will help you grab that brass ring with an iron fist.

Michael D. Peters

Securing the C Level

Getting, Keeping, or Reclaiming that Executive Title

Contents

Part 1: So you want to be a corporate executive?....... 1

Chapter 2: The Direct and Indirect Whereabouts
of Point B:................................3
    What is your Mantra?.......................5
    Your personal marching orders...................6

Fundamental Rule 1: Look Before You Leap............25
    Market research..........................27
    The power of the network....................32
    Be realistic.............................37
    Interviewing............................40
    Correct interpretations......................47
    Work life balance.........................50
    Word on the street indicators, if they are available ... 51
    Get promises in writing......................54

Part 2: Now that you have arrived...................57

Fundamental Rule 2: Measure Twice, Cut Once
    Lying in wait............................63
    Corporate culture.........................65
    Complain about nothing even if you have
        something to complain about................68
    Communication style.......................72
    Leadership style 78
    Peer Group.............................87
    Be wary of possible competition.................88

Political collaborations, even symbolic ones 91
Get organized quickly 95
Consider creating a personal brand 96
Saying less is more. 99

Part 3: Trouble in Paradise 101
Clash of the Corporate Culture 101
The "Sucker Punch" 102
You might regret the words that come
out of your mouth 107

Fundamental Rule 3: Loose Lips Sink Ships 107
Don't paint a target on yourself willingly 109
Don't tell war stories in an effort to fit in
Social media 110
You know what they say about assumptions 116

Part 4: Turning adversity into triumph 119

Fundamental Rule 4: "You never know when you're
auditioning." 119
Have a good cover story. 120
I'm honored by your fear. 124
Credential building. 127
Flowchart strategy 128
Eyes on the industry 131
Search agents. 133
Knowledge is power. 134
Salary surveys 134
Reconnaissance on the competition. 135
Understand the law 137
Contractual rights. 140

Words of wisdom 143

Closing comments 145

I'm here for you! 147

About the author 149

References 151

Part 1

So you want to be a corporate executive?

At this very moment, you may be at the proverbial crossroads in your career, the point that every single executive level career person reaches just prior to making that leap. I was there myself once. I recall several facets of consideration that helped shape my decision and that provided me with the information I needed to build up the courage to make the jump that would signal a paradigm shift in my career and lifestyle. With just a limited number of executive positions available, you may be asking yourself: What do I need to do to increase my chances of success in securing a piece of this rare commodity? What are the differences between an executive interviewing process other traditional job interviews? How is compensation going to change, if at all, to what I am accustomed to now? Believe me, it is a completely different world you are about to explore and it helps to take a personal guide with you. Your journey will become more enjoyable, more efficient, more sustainable, and more rewarding by doing so.

So many questions and I had few sources of information available to me to help make the decisions necessary for my success. If I had other executives willing to discuss my questions and share their experiences, I would have been better prepared for joining the executive ranks. I am here to serve as your guide and career mentor on your journey towards earning one of those coveted elite positions within the corporate structure. You can examine the organizational structure of any corporation and it will be painfully obvious to you that the executive ranks occupy probably only one percent of the hierarchy. I remember watching news programs during the American corporate accounting scandals of the 1990s and the reports revealing the compensation levels of all of these executives. While I abhor the criminal activity which was the focus of the reports, I also came to the conclusion that the criminal or questionable activity executed by these few did not represent the entire corporate spectrum. How did these people rise to these elite executive ranks, I wondered, and how do I get there? With such a spectacular compensation gap between the ranks, how do I bridge that gap? Why work for the man when you can *be* the man, right? Have you had any of these same questions?

Whatever your area of expertise, whatever you executive level focus may be, I'm going to help guide you towards career success. You will gain both professional and personal satisfaction in getting that first executive position. You will gain recognition as an expert executive professional, while also honing your leadership skills. Your career will be forever changed for the better by applying solid principles and recommendations found in these pages.

Chapter 2

The Direct and Indirect Whereabouts of Point B:

"Do not go where the path may lead; go instead where there is no path and leave a trail"
- Ralph Waldo Emerson

A good business colleague and friend once told me, "Dude, you just took off like a rocket!" This comment was made just a few years following my departure from the same company he remained in employment with until the global economic turmoil of 2010. In just a few short years I went from being a peer with a similar resume and similar credentials, laboring away in the same size cubicle, to being the chief information security officer of a very large financial institution with a very nice corner office, reserved parking spot, and personal assistant. I've never truly appreciated the metaphor he used. Not that I don't appreciate his intended meaning, but in my mind, taking off like a rocket suggested to me that a person expends a lot of energy to move very quickly, only to sputter out and subsequently crash and burn in a fiery heap of debris and human wreckage. For me, this is a visual I don't care to be associated with. What I have in mind is far more sustainable.

Does this fiery crash and burn sound like the career path you want to take? Wouldn't a more durable and sustainable career path be more rewarding? Do I want to be a shooting star quickly forgotten or do I want to be this point of illumination that others around me appreciate, share in, and remember long after I am gone? I immediately considered these questions while I contemplated my friend's metaphor. How do I achieve and surpass my peer group effectively without leaving behind me a trail of career wreckage? How do I create something worthy of remembering for the right reasons, not the notorious ones?

The effective Point B on life's map for each and every one of us who are walking the earth today; for all those that came before us and for all those that will come after us is that destination. It's the point of separation, of delineation that compels one person to rise above a group of peers, above a cast of millions in reality, to achieve more, to accomplish more in life than most people do. I'm convinced that personal achievement and success is largely a function of our deliberate, concerted effort to earn the right credentials, work with the right people, pay our essential dues, and know where you intend to go so that time and opportunities are not wasted. It's so easy to get distracted along the way.

How many times have you been on a road trip going to Point B when you are faced with two questions? The first question is, "How long will I need to drive and what is the most direct route to get there?" The other question is, probably, "Do I want to take any detours on my way to Point B?" Well we certainly know that these questions have something to do with our personal sense of urgency, or desire to arrive at our intended destination on schedule. Maybe we are not in any hurry and meandering is the way we travel. Meandering is a result of two factors really. One factor is that we lack resolution in our life and Point B has never been properly defined or considered. Are you content with drifting through life without a roadmap, without having a good idea of where you are going? I derive peace and contentment with having a plan. In doing so, I am able to eliminate obstacles and stress through the organization, determination, execution, protection, and satisfaction that comes from a well-conceived plan.

What is your Mantra?

"I will bludgeon my way to victory!" – Michael D. Peters

I rather prefer the expression "I will bludgeon my way to victory!" as opposed to taking off like a rocket. I coined my personal mantra expression many years ago and it declares my determined, persistent effort until I succeed. In any battle, you hack your way through or around obstacles until there are no more challenges and you achieve success. In battle, as in life, you may get knocked down or thrown off course. However, knowing what your objectives are will keep you focused and true to the goals you have set your sights upon. Defining what your measure of success will be will help you identify objectives and subordinate goals you will pass as the milestones from your life plan unfold on your way to achieving your goals. I guarantee you will achieve more in less time when you define goals for most endeavors, be it to secure that executive position, earn a graduate degree, or even to just lead a good life just by making a silent declaration to yourself and resolving to see your plan through to the end. Accountability is very important to success so sharing your roadmap with other people will promote accountability and success because, after all, we have our pride to cultivate as well as the perceptions of others who matter.

Your personal marching orders

"Good plans shape good decisions. That's why good planning helps to make elusive dreams come true."
- Lester R. Bittel

It is important to know where you are going or where you want to be in order to arrive at your destination in the most efficient way possible. The proverbial point B, describes your destination. If you set out on life's road without a map or reasonable instructions on how to get to your destination, the likelihood of getting lost or delaying your arrival at your destination exponentially increases. Why should your career plan be any different? The basic building blocks of your Point B roadmap consist of both long-term objectives and short-term objectives. We will gradually explore each of those in-depth.

What are your long-term objectives? At this moment, what career positional goal do you aspire to achieve? You may have, as I did, more than one long-term goal in mind. For example, I would consider there are three facets to occupational pursuits that should be considered. They are as an employee, as an employer, and as an independent consultant. I have traversed all three of these occupational options at various points in my career, depending on my critical objectives and my ultimate goals. . Some of our long-term goals require exposure to certain business models or corporate cultures to acquire some of those softer skills and experiences that many employers find desirable in the executives they hire. I recall on many occasions during those important interviews where my diversity of experiences was an asset that gave me an advantage over other candidates.

What are short-term objectives? These major goals will consist of smaller components such as soft skills you will need to acquire, business experiences, and credentials that round out the whole package you are working on to achieve your goals. From a pure credential standpoint, your ultimate career goals will also help you make decisions for certifications and academic degree programs you pursue. In my situation, my executive level career aspirations would put me in a seat around the boardroom table where my peer group would be a collection of other business professionals. Understanding that my dominating talents are technological in focus was important, but in order to effectively contribute to enterprise business objectives, other business skills were required. In my case, an MBA with a technological management emphasis was ideal to satisfy the technology executive positions I desired, but also enabled me to stand shoulder to shoulder with the other executives who reported to the CEO. I'll explore this in more detail with you later.

I'd like to distill down a little bit further some of the core elements or concepts that will help you achieve your executive goals more effectively. There are five essential concepts that we will explore together. They are organization, determination, execution, protection, and satisfaction. We will now explore these together in brief.

- Organization
- Determination
- Execution
- Protection
- Satisfaction

- **Organization:** I happen to be a very visual person so developing visual aids patents is very important to me. I personally believe that when we commit our ideas and plans to paper, we commit ourselves to success. If you stop to consider our society and the way we commit ourselves to organizations, or agreements, or promises, all of these concepts are captured on paper. The simple reason for this is to memorialize our commitment in a visual way that encourages us and others to conduct ourselves honorably according to the letter of the law and agreement. Given the example, why would you not commit your goals and aspirations to paper? In my case, and I'll elaborate more later on in this book, I use a combination of visual aids to help me stay committed to the ideas and plans I have resolved myself to complete. For my career path, I have chosen a simple flowchart with decision points and measurable objectives that I color-code to assist me in visualizing my career focus and success. For simple tasks, I always use task lists that frequently contain critical path elements, again, to help me visualize the task at hand and the sequence of events that must occur for my success to follow. Finally, I utilize more formal outlines to capture and articulate in more detail about ideas and concepts. This free-form does not have any critical path illustrations or completion dates or any other time to completion information and is designed strictly to maintain and organize my thoughts about possible goals I will set for myself in the future. As you read further, I'd like you to consider setting strategic career goals for yourself as well as a reasonable but aggressive timeline for achieving these goals.

All things worth doing in this life take time. It is important to establish reasonable goals for ourselves. I'm not referring to those hollow New Year's resolutions that are loosely constructed and easily get pushed out of the way because life happens. The fact of the matter is that life does happen and we must prepare ourselves for it every day. It is in our very nature, and our DNA, to prepare for diversity, for change, for opportunity. It is also in our nature, to procrastinate, become complacent, to become comfortable with our current achievements. This comfortable situation is an illusion, is short-lived, and is only a fleeting moment before it too passes and our next challenge presents itself to us.

There are only two approaches to dealing with change in our lives and the first is through a proactive response, and the other is a purely reactive response. The reactive response is quite simply our response to changes impacting our lives that we have very little control over and are not necessarily foreseen by us. A much more positive response would be to address life in a proactive manner. A proactive response demonstrates personal readiness and that you have a plan, that you are responsible, and are reasonably prepared to handle change that will inevitably occur in your life.

Set reasonable goals for yourself. You already established what Point B looks like on your personal career progression project plan, right? What other important goals should be placed in your plan so that you can achieve your career goals within a reasonable amount of time? Decide what these tasks should be, do your research into what it takes to accomplish these tasks in a reasonable amount of time, make a decision for yourself as to when you expect to complete the work front needed to complete these goals. I would recommend weighing what is most important to you such as your family, your other commitments, or any other activity that consumes your time and make a determination as to what takes priority and reverse-engineer those activities effectively, distilling a reasonable timeline for yourself. My natural tendency is to be a little more aggressive with the tasks that will provide significant gains in my career, ultimately benefiting myself and those who depend on me. My other hobbies, personal interests, and diversions will get put on ice until I am able to free up my time once again, which will occur following the completion of a task I have a priority upon. I frequently tell other people around me to "work smarter, not harder," which is an integral theme and an important element you should depend on while working through your personal career progression project plan. Be able to consolidate tasks that satisfy the requirements of some of the other goals you may have on the horizon. If you've taken the time to do simple analysis, the common elements will be readily apparent to you.

Word of caution from someone who practices what he preaches, you will want to include a little extra time in your schedule to accommodate unforeseen events that require your attention. Or perhaps you'll need a little down time to regroup as we all find it necessary to do from time to time. If your expectations of time are not reasonable this will inevitably lead to personal frustration and potentially resentment from those people around you who also are vying for your time and attention. One of the very difficult tasks indeed does come from those people around you who must also adapt to your new schedule so it is important, and only fair, that everyone supports your new endeavor to achieve a loftier position in life or on the job. I always make sure that the people who depend on me receive quality time from me and I strive to have a healthy work life balance. The key to success is in the reasonable and appropriate scheduling of your time and planning your activities.

- Organization
- **Determination**
- Execution
- Protection
- Satisfaction

- **Determination**: Sacrifice everything except what truly matters. For me, this would be my family. I will devote a healthy amount of quality time to each member of my immediate family. This is not a one-way responsibility. This endeavor to achieve our career goals should provide every member of our family with tangible benefits. Otherwise, what is the point of working so hard just to leave human wreckage in your aspirations' wake? You all achieve great things and accomplish your goals simply by having a good plan, a reasonable strategy to accomplish your goals, and the determination to see these tasks through to the end. "I will bludgeon my way to victory" is the phrase that I use to remind myself that I must remain vigilant, persistent, and most determined if I want to achieve the goals that I have envisioned for myself. If I don't master these challenges, who will? If I don't press on, who else will or why should they?

Determination is an admirable quality, and when wielded properly assists us in achieving greater things. It is quite easy to lose sight of the things around us if we become absorbed or otherwise overly determined. I would recommend periodic sanity checks, simple conversations you may have with yourself, to validate your decisions again. The benefit from second-wind validation is fresh resolve or perhaps directional changes to adapt to some unforeseen obstacle that will reduce your effective progress.

- Organization
- Determination
- **Execution**
- Protection
- Satisfaction

- **Execution:** What are you waiting for, an invitation, gold nuggets to fall from heaven, or someone to do it for you? You have a plan, a roadmap that illustrates what you defined as Point B, so now go execute your plan! We make our opportunities in life. Sheer willpower and tuned observation will take you anywhere. You must know where you are going in order to have even a basic clue on how you will get there. You must look before you leap in order to spot and grab onto opportunities that emerge, but also to avoid temptations that derail our progress and success. Some situations appear as opportunities but are really distractions to progress and success.

- Organization
- Determination
- Execution
- **Protection**
- Satisfaction

- **Protection:** In my experience, this is the hardest point to master. Paradigm shifts always make a segment of the population uncomfortable. This resistance to change intrigues me. Advancements we collectively make in thought, in process, in technology, in philosophy, and so forth brings a positive facet and a negative one. Social media is no exception. I, for one, strive to embrace change rather than fear change. What should be an obvious fact to everyone is that we cannot and should not attempt to stifle change, but learn about it, become leaders in it, and do our best to manage it wisely. This change philosophy is applicable to the individual and global collective equally.

Anyone can steer the ship, but it takes a leader to chart the course. A healthy balance of optimism and realism, intuition and planning, confidence and fact can be very difficult to achieve. A successful person or leader will do their best to eradicate certain weaknesses within themselves, such as the fear of change, or mitigate the fear of uncertainty by formulating a reasonable plan under which to push forward. A leader cannot, however, eradicate their own lack of imagination or ignorance. It may be mitigated by surrounding yourself with those people whose attributes you might leverage, but pity the person who is ignorant and does not possess an imagination.

I hope to avoid turning myself into a time capsule or walking into that proverbial cave, never to come out again. The world is much too interesting to shut my mind off to it. Kick me if I start to exhibit signs of doing so, please. Protecting what you have worked for so diligently and carefully is the best advice here. Never be deterred by obstacles, never go willingly or quietly away into the back pages of history, and always protect what matters most.

- Organization
- Determination
- Execution
- Protection
- **Satisfaction**

- **Satisfaction:** If you skate on thin ice, you run the increased risk of falling through the ice. If you cannot find some level of satisfaction in your success and achievements, you are at risk of falling through the ice. Think of ice as that layer of success we skate on, showcasing our abilities to all of the spectators watching us. That layer of ice may be very thin due to our limited level of job maturity and required expertise. This is a situation that most people are faced with when they grab that first C-Level position. Everyone is a rookie at least once in their life. I felt, rightfully so, like a rookie with each successive rung I climbed up on the corporate ladder. With each new level of achievement, I had a brand new set of experiences to master. It takes time for every newly-acquired skill to mature. It takes time and learned experiences to become the sage within your career space. That maturity can be analogized as that ice you skate upon. Thin ice is unstable, untested, and it presents risks to those that would prematurely test it. In my career, being content is the hardest thing to do. I've had to learn to objectively consider my options and desires. I've had to learn to avoid impulsive decisions. Just because someone just waived an apple in front of my face does not mean that I cannot resist taking a bite.

Designing your personal roadmap for success may sound like a feel-good exercise, but don't dwell on the softer side of what I am suggesting you do and instead approach it like a project plan. One fact that quickly emerged for me was when I planned a project and captured major steps that would be required to successfully complete my mission: It occurred to me, why should I not treat my career progression in a similar fashion? I certainly have defined goals or deliverables at the end signifying success, right? I certainly have keystone components to collect or achieve along the project timeline that I consider necessary to achieve project plan success, so why would I treat career progression any differently? What I've been able to achieve using this technique is to reach my goals sooner than I ever expected and to do so. And I have done it more expeditiously than many in peer group.

My personal career progression project plan resembles a basic flow chart. I started with the only three possible input paths I could think of, and they are as an employee, as an employer, and as a free agent or consultant. My next step was to define what the "perfect" end result would be. Keep in mind that as you evolve and develop over time, your career progression project plan should also evolve, adapting to your changing needs as well as market changes you perceive influencing your career progression project plan. To give you an example of what I am referring to, once upon a time, I thought that the ultimate career-end state would be as the chief information security officer to some large corporation. I placed this career goal at the very end of my career progression project plan along with an estimated income potential for that position. You have probably heard the expression, "if I knew then what I know now," and when I made this goal originally, my perceptions about what it would take to achieve this goal are somewhat different from today. It has evolved with me, matured with me. That career progression project plan has been updated over time, however, it still resembles the plan I created years ago.

The next step in creating your personal career progression project plan is to add significant elements that will be necessary, or most likely necessary to achieve success in the career path you have selected. These items should be focused upon academic and credential-building achievements such as certifications relevant to your particular career field. I suggest that these goals be driven by the job market. When you look at a job posting listed on some Internet career site, there will be minimum requirements to be considered as a viable candidate. Your first round of personal career progression project plan goals should be to secure the minimums first. In my personal situation, to be the chief information security officer, I needed a bachelor of science degree from an accredited university in some technical field such as computer science and I needed to have at least one major information security certification such as the certified information systems security professional (CISSP) ™. These job listings will of course refer to experience, but that is not something you will illustrate on your personal career progression project plan.

Be keenly cognizant of external entities that may potentially threaten your continued progress or incumbency. I've been keenly aware of the "whipper-snappers" are out there. They are younger and work for less. They are the fresh faces eager to replace you or successfully compete for the position you are vying for. The one important element you possess is experience. The whipper-snappers will never be able to match your experience, however, there is a tipping point at which employers will weigh between the premium prices that are paid with a complete employee package versus one that is a reasonable compromise. I use the word "reasonable" to suggest that value is not sacrificed, but it may be the downside to bargain shopping; you absolutely get what you paid for. I would hope a competent hiring manager is performing an impromptu risk analysis on hiring decisions. In my experience, however, this is far from the norm and more the exception.

Once you have accomplished the entry-level components on your personal career progression project plan, don't sit on your laurels. Continue growing, continue stretching, and continue adding value to your credential portfolio. The more tangible value you add to your credential war chest, the more difficult it will be for your competition to keep pace with you and win. Leadership develops daily, not in a day. As I have already stated, there is a tipping point between the competing candidate's credentials and their compensation expectations.

I try to impress upon my associates, especially those whom I lead, the importance of becoming a life learner. This concept is, as the title implies, a life-long enriching commitment. . An epiphany strikes when you learn something new. Suddenly your intellectual world became larger. It takes time to culture your intellect, your personality, your leadership abilities, and who you are holistically. This takes a plan. Personally, my plan is visual in nature, consisting of a flowchart that depicts my career, education, and lifework aspirations, neatly organized on paper. Like me, it too evolves. Becoming a successful leader is a lot like investing successfully in the market. If your hope is to make a fortune in a single day, you're not going to be very successful. I encourage you to embrace a similar approach. You will find that through thoughtful self-examination, you will grow stronger, more proficient, more self-aware, and closer to becoming a better person.

I make it a habit of investing time in those people who I lead or mentor or influence in some way. I believe that those people who do this inspire a culture of personal growth and leadership development that becomes recognized and valued by the same people. I've witnessed explosive growth from these teams, companies, or prescribers. Commit to it. It's not going to transpire overnight, but good things and positive results rarely do anyway. In my career, there have been a few people along the way who I've admired for different reasons, but I always remember my mentors the most. For example, Mark Miller, the founding partner of CriticalPath Partners, is a driving force within the consulting space, a colleague, and a good friend. Once upon a time, I worked for Mark as a security and compliance consultant. I'm not sure why he took an interest in me, it's probably just in his nature, but with Mark, you always felt like you were important. It is this type of mentoring that matters to your employees and they will always appreciate it; they might even write about you in books.

There are, of course, some individuals who do not appreciate your investment in them and this will become apparent to you in short order. Your resources are finite so use them wisely and as the expression goes, don't cast pearls before swine.

Fundamental Rule 1: Look Before You Leap

"The leader is one who climbs the tallest tree, surveys the entire situation, and yells, 'Wrong jungle!'"
- Stephen Covey

A clever person will pursue alternate paths to obtain the desired end result. Look before you leap. This is a subject I've written about, blogged about, and spoken about during my career, but more so during the latter part of my leadership experiences thus far. I refer to this as the "look before you leap" facet of leadership. This happens to be a leadership trait that I believe anyone in a position of authority should be able to grasp and apply quite easily. It is fundamentally prudent to know where you intend to be going and, within reason, what you are getting yourself into. The alternative is essentially volunteering to put blinders on, accepting ignorance, walking with your eyes closed through life. The more unfamiliar the territory, the newer the organization is to you, and the better it is to look before you leap into uncharted waters. I'll be the first to encourage you to definitely march on, grow, discover, seize the day, but, in the interest of self-preservation, go forth with open eyes and an open mind.

Another facet concerns natural selection. I am a significant proponent of natural selection. We live, love, and work in a tribe, community, collective, or global environment, dependent, in part, on those who came before and for the benefit of our species, those that will come after.

We do our species a serious disservice by overly supporting those less-than-desirable traits evolution has so effectively eradicated. I'd even go as far as to suggest that we are slowly killing ourselves with kindness. Some people I lead want to work hard, contribute, and achieve more, while others are the complete opposite. If I spend more time promoting and supporting less desirable attributes, I reinforce those attributes. Conversely, ideally, I should strive to identify and reinforce the positive attributes instead. Part of our success in business, in life in general, is a direct result of certain people who push themselves, bolster support from the organization, and ultimately raise the standards, the knowledge, the bar, and expectations for everyone. There is no point in living if we are not learning, growing, loving, and striving.

I suppose that some of my economic training will shine through right now but, since economics is not one of my strong suits, please excuse my rudimentary comments. The division of labor is the breakdown of labor into specific, circumscribed tasks for maximum efficiency. The fragmentation or reduction of human activity into a separated laborious effort is the practical root of alienation and basic specialization which makes civilization appear and develop. The specialization and concentration of the workers on their single sub-tasks often leads to greater skill and greater productivity on their particular sub-tasks than would be achieved by the same number of workers, each carrying out the original broad task. These principles speak to the point that I'm trying to articulate. Specifically, there is a fixed difference between those of us with natural abilities to lead and strategize effectively, and those with competent, average ability to manage tasks but not strategy, and the vast majority of the remaining population whose cog specializations keep humanity's machine running smoothly. It is very important to be at peace with one's strengths and weaknesses. Leaders need to get out of their comfort zone a bit. Don't abandon your strong suit, but stretch yourself a bit.

"Some people are just cogs in a machine while others are the machine." – Michael D. Peters

The point I'm about to make specifically addresses fundamental rule number one. If you are intent on joining the executive ranks, you must be prepared to reach a little higher than you may be accustomed to reaching, figuratively speaking. As you plot your trajectory toward your goal, there will be a few fundamental activities you will want to invest time in in an effort to cultivate these activities. It is very important to approach these things with as much professionalism as possible, which is where the look before you leap analogy comes into play. You wouldn't go skydiving without understanding how a parachute worked, would you? It would make no sense to blindly apply for new opportunities without understanding the standard rules of engagement, or without being knowledgeable about many of the standard practices that go along with making application for that executive position. There is very little similarity in competing for a more subordinate position within an organization and that of a senior executive position within the same company. We will review many of these issues and situations together and I will lift the veil for you, increasing your opportunities and prospects.

Market research

Knowledge is power. How many times have you heard that one? All large companies know that fact and devote lots of resources into research to gain the knowledge they need to be competitive. Companies commit extensive resources to conducting market research before selling their products and services. Some large companies employ or enlist huge information centers where they have a full complement of professional librarians and researchers who are able to access information on clients, competitors, and customers. This is an important fact to observe. The amount of advanced knowledge you have about a potential employer, and on the industry in which you hope to work or rise up the corporate ladder, can give you a competitive edge. This recommendation pertains to not only making your initial contact with employers, but also going on interviews. In addition, having information on a company is also very valuable when it comes to effectively evaluating a job offer. There are, of course, some organizations you should refuse for a variety of reasons.

Having advanced rudimentary knowledge about a potential employer gives you an intelligent edge over the competition. It is important and prudent to learn how to do company research and find the resources you can use to research most companies, including Securities and Exchange Commission (SEC) filings, business directories, and various news sources. Search engines are your friend in this space. It never ceases to amaze me when a potential employee candidate sits before me for an interview and doesn't have a basic fundamental understanding of what the company's business provides. There are so many publically-available resources on the Internet alone today; don't waste a great research tool. In my experience, employers appreciate candidates who understand why they have been called in for an interview and have meaningful comments about the company. Before going on an interview is the time to do extensive research. Being armed with an arsenal of information can give you an edge over your competition, as you will be able to answer any questions the employer may ask you about the company. It is not unusual to be asked the question, "What do you know about us?" It will also enable you to ask intelligent questions when you are given the opportunity, as job candidates are offered to do toward the end of the interview. Just as researching clients gives corporations the ability to individually target sales presentations, knowing your potential employer will help you target your presentation to them.

When you're searching for that next great job, the one that signifies to the world that you have arrived, you'll want to learn as much about potential employers as possible. Knowing the financial standing of a company can help you decide whether to make a commitment to that company. If a company is on shaky financial ground, you must evaluate whether you want to stake your future there. By keeping up with business news, you can learn in which direction a company is headed. This advanced knowledge will give you a competitive edge and also help you when evaluating a potential offer from the company. I would advise keeping up with industry-specific business news. It is very important to your career, whether you're currently employed or searching for work. There are many tools available to assist you in this endeavor, such as syndication feeds that plug into your e-mail client, browser, or standalone syndication clients. I believe that it is as if you are keeping your fingers on the pulse of whatever business vertical you are interested in pursuing.

Even if money isn't what gives you the most job satisfaction, no one can argue its importance. Most people, outside of the independently wealthy, need a certain amount of money to pay the bills. Most of us also want to make sure we are being paid what we're worth and what is the going rate for jobs similar to ours. It is an unpleasant reality to discover that your predecessor perhaps commanded a much larger salary, or that the industry median salary far exceeds yours. It is a reality that dampens the spirits and spoils the satisfaction level you get from this otherwise great position. It's important to find out what others are making for related work in the same industry, and in the same geographic region. You can start gathering this information by looking at salary surveys and other occupational information that are readily and freely available on the Internet. Salary surveys are useful tools when you are choosing a career or looking for a job. One factor to consider when choosing a career is the salary you can hope to earn. When searching for a new job or considering a new job offer, salary information can help you make sure you will earn what you're worth on the open market. Keep in mind that aside from base salary, there are other aspects of the job that may appeal to you, and you can certainly try to negotiate the offer. These facts should be well-defined and rehearsed in your mind prior to that interview so that your responses are natural and confident.

Try not to get trapped into the typical question all recruiters and employers ask during the pre-qualification phase of employment, and that is the "what is your current salary" question. The conundrum is that you want to be honest but in doing so you set the stage for limiting your earning potential, which of course leads to job dissatisfaction, a condition both employee and employer should avoid. My advice to you is to conduct a salary survey for your targeted position. Keep in mind that logistics and business verticals will play an important role is your efforts to determine what the fair market rate would be, given your credentials and other factors these surveys account for. A little knowledge in advance of that recruiter's cold call or your targeted effort will help you provide a fair answer to that question. It is acceptable to not reveal your current salary level and even to provide a false answer just to protect your financial position. Recruiters typically target a 10 percent increase in your base salary alone to entice you, which is great unless this position happens to significantly exceed your current one, financially speaking.

Another market research angle you should examine is the knowledge that most publicly-held companies are required to file in corporate reporting documents with the

Securities and Exchange Commission. The document familiar to most people is the annual report, which must be sent to each shareholder as well. The annual report contains corporate financial information as well as other points of interest. Companies must report on their corporate officers, new acquisitions, and lines of business. The annual report is usually a professionally-published document resembling a magazine or brochure. The corporate information is presented in such a way that is most appealing to shareholders. Annual reports can be obtained by calling the investor relations department of the company in which you are interested.

Something I learned while earning an MBA was that a more rudimentary corporate report document is the 10-K. It contains the same information that is required in the annual report. This year-end report must be filed three months after the end of the corporation's fiscal year. For example, if you are researching a particular company in February of 2012, the most recent 10-K or annual report you most likely will be able to obtain may be the 2010 report. That is when the 10-Q report comes in handy. The 10-Q report is a quarterly report that also must be filed with the SEC. Although there is some time-lag between the end of a quarter and the date at which a report must be filed, it will help you bridge the gap some. The annual report, 10-K, and 10-Q should provide you with the information you need. Before we begin to discuss the types of resources we can use to access company information, we must first understand the accessibility of this information. Not all companies are required to make financial information easily available to the public. Let's begin by discussing what companies are required to disclose this information. Please note that this information pertains to United States law only. It should be used to determine how you will conduct your research and should not be used as a guide for filing with the United States Securities and Exchange Commission.

Just a note on the difference between publicly-held and privately-held companies is that a publicly-held company has outside shareholders who have a financial interest in the company. Not every company with shareholders is required to disclose their financial information though. A company must file with the United States Securities and Exchange Commission (S.E.C.) if its securities are traded in interstate commerce, the company has more than one million dollars in assets, and/or there is a class of equity security held by 500 or more shareholders. Conversely, privately-held companies are like the description implies, private. Financial information about those companies is often kept private as well. Occasionally, these companies disclose some financial information, but they are not required to do so. Therefore, accessing information on privately-held companies is sometimes difficult, but not impossible. I can attest that as a security practitioner myself, you can generally count on information leaks from just about any organization.

The power of the network

Various experts have long stressed the importance of networking to one's career growth. Through networking we can learn about job opportunities, particularly those we wouldn't have had access to otherwise. However, job searching should not be the primary focus of your networking efforts. Your network can prove to be a very useful tool when it comes to other aspects of your career. Your contacts can give you advice and provide information. There are just a few simple words of advice that will help you maximize the benefits of networking.

First, everyone you know is a potential member of your personal network. When it comes to professional networking everyone you know can be a useful contact. While someone may not be directly involved in your field, he or she may know another person who is.

Second, a network is reciprocal in nature. You should be willing, at times, to ask for assistance and be willing to offer assistance from your network. The network doesn't exist only for your benefit. You should be willing to offer your help to others as well.

Third, the network is not only used for employment opportunities. Many people have the misconception that networking is only for job hunting. They attempt to utilize it only when looking for work. The reality is that if you only get in touch with your network of contacts when you are looking for work, your network may dry up. Your network contacts may also perceive you negatively as the "that person who's always looking for a new job" or that you are a user and not a mutual benefiter. This connotation may certainly be misplaced but is negative and you should certainly avoid being associated with it. It is advisable to check in with your contacts periodically. Find out what they're up to and let them know what is happening with your career. It will be much easier to track someone down after not talking to them for a couple of months than it will be after being out of touch for a year or longer.

Fourth and lastly, thank your network contacts for their help. Even those folks who are just well-wishers, a simple thank-you will go a long way to building relationships. When one of your network contacts gives you advice or provides you with a job lead, do not forget to send that person a thank you message. You can use e-mail, postal services, or the telephone to accomplish this. I like to use professional networks such as *Linkedin.com* to convey my thank-you messages. Not only are you announcing to a potentially very large network of members and contacts, but the publically-conveyed words of appreciation will be noticed and received well. It may also provide unforeseen benefits to your contacts that will further culture your reciprocal networking experience for the future.

There are many other resources that you may leverage, some you may find more unconventional that I still recommend you examine. I obtained examples of this from one of my business colleagues, Nancy Fox, who owns the business and marketing site, TheBusinessFox.com and helps professionals and entrepreneurs develop marketing strategies. Many of these same principles are quite adaptable to your own executive level aspirations. Knowledge is power and it is wise to consider sage advice wherever you may find it.

If I offered you any cautionary advice regarding the usage of networks like the ones I've described above, it would be to remain predictably consistent with your activity level on the same networking sites. For example, if you rarely maintained or cultivate your online presence and one day you decide to begin looking for a new opportunity, the behavioral difference will of course be displayed online at updates made available to all the individuals within your network, signaling a very noticeable change. If you are currently employed, coworkers or your supervisor, who are naturally within your network of associates, will suddenly be aware that your status is changed. If you begin networking with executive recruiters, these relationships will be displayed also to your current employment relationships. This activity might potentially create unnecessary tension in your current employment situation. Try to cultivate an air of unpredictability. All humans are essentially creatures of habit with an insatiable need to see familiarity in other people's actions. Your predictability gives them a sense of control which you should use for strategic advantage not only as a promotional advantage, but also as a leadership tool. The converse to predictability is to be deliberately unpredictable. Behavior that seems to have no consistency or purpose will keep others off-balance, and they wear themselves out trying to explain and interpret your moves. Taken to an extreme, however, this strategy can intimidate and terrorize. I think another interesting aspect to predictability is that being unpredictable actually lends itself towards personal security. If we lead predictable lives it gives others with malice the opportunity to take advantage of our predictability. The key element or ingredient is really discretion. By not visibly declaring your intentions, you inform fewer people around you of your intentions, lending itself a facade of unpredictability.

The best advice I will offer you is that you should remain consistently predictable. Certainly add relationships to your network such as those executive recruiters, but also add other employees from your current employer. While the human resource department or your boss may ask the question of whether or not you are looking for new job due to the fact that you just added an executive recruiter to your network, you can calmly point out that you also added other business associates to your network. It also doesn't hurt to tell them that on occasion you get contacted by recruiters and accepting their connection requests is the polite thing to do.

If you have an interest in publishing articles, writing commentary, maintaining a blog or wiki, publications, or participating in network forum discussions, I would highly encourage you, assuming the content is appropriate, to cross-link these other activities with your professional networking sites. For example, my personal blog, MichaelPeters.org, is configured to automatically update my Twitter.com, Linkedin.com, Facebook.com, and Feedburner.com sites with the content from my blog. I always say, "Work smarter, not harder," and this is a great example. It is a valuable activity to demonstrate your relevance and subject-matter savvy to potential employers and other potential opportunities through your personally-maintained websites. I frequently write business and IT-related articles for *Technorati.com* and then republish through my blog. In the executive space, some of my favorite publications that provide cutting-edge news and information relevant to your C-level aspirations are CFO, CIO, and my favorite, CSO Magazine. They all have smartphone applications now so you have these resources at your fingertips whenever you have a chance. They are great resources that can help you to stay current and also allows you to publish within. You never know when you're auditioning right? You want to maintain a professional façade and publish material that is thoughtful and well-constructed in order to showcase some of your softer skills and subject-matter prowess.

Depending how prolific you are, I would recommend pacing your publishing activity so that you have "fresh meat" available about once a week. This performs two functions. First, search engines maintain a certain cataloging and indexing frequency you want to take advantage of to maximize your syndication efforts. A cautionary note, however, is that by taking a shape, by having a visible plan, a personal brand, you open yourself up to public commentary. You do have the power to control many aspects of this activity. Instead of taking a form for your adversaries to grasp, keep yourself adaptable, agile, and on the move. Accept the fact that nothing is certain and nothing is fixed. The best way to protect yourself is to be a fluid and formless as water and never bet on stability or lasting order; everything changes. Several quotes come to mind instantly, like "Nothing lasts forever," "What is old is new," and "The more things change, the more they stay the same." I think the point is in order to remain vibrant and relevant, we must remain agile. Complacency comes way too easy to humanity; we seem to only respond expeditiously, unfortunately to duress. Why is logic not the driver? I refuse to wait for death, wasting away in a decrepit shell. No, I think death must catch me and only because I burned out like a flaming comet across the finish line, completely spending the fire within.

Secondly, this consistency becomes valuable within your professional network projecting a certain heartbeat. Your associations and contacts will be notified of your activity on a consistent basis and this keeps you fresh, or in all of their minds. Believe in yourself and your vision and be prepared to constantly defend those beliefs. Only then will innovation and inspiration flourish and only then will you be able to find or attract an awesome employment opportunity.

Jane Cranston, and executive career coach who has written, among many things, a publication called *Top 3 Job Search Mistakes Smart People Make*, offers some solid advice to folks like you and I, such as leveraging the power of your network. Obviously, I couldn't agree more.

Be realistic

Setting expectations is very much a part of the planning process on your way to the top. You need to develop a realistic plan that is based upon attainable criteria to achieve success and satisfaction. As you have developed your personal career-progression plan, you now have a pretty good idea of what Point B looks like and now you need to make certain that all of your bases are covered. Take some time to examine job descriptions for positions that interest you and they will tell you quite clearly what that particular company's expectations are and what you would need in order to be considered a viable candidate. For example, most executive positions today require at least a bachelor's degree in an appropriate field of study. You may notice that the same job description also contains the phrase "master's degree preferred," which means the employer is seeking candidates who are more academically progressive. As I recall reading job descriptions during the previous ten-year period of time, there was rarely a reference to a master's degree and typically, the job description read "bachelor's degree preferred." Obviously the bar is being raised and corporate expectations are increasing, which I think is a great trend, but one that you must consider carefully as you prepare yourself to joining the executive ranks. Your personal career-progression plan should include academic and certification pursuits that will keep your credentials fresh and progressively ahead of your competition as potential employers gradually raise their expectations and hire executive members of their staff. You will want to be thoughtful about certifications. Too many will make you appear like a certification junkie, which diminishes your brand. Pair this with frequent job changes and now you have a liability to contend with. Choose wisely.

It is certainly a balancing act that you must strive for between obtaining enough exposure to different corporate cultures, business models, and business verticals. Too much diversity will not be looked at favorably by some potential employers; conversely, some others will look at you as the well-rounded candidate. It is important, especially in your more junior, pre-executive portion of your career, to gain this exposure. It is very similar to academically working your way through a bachelor's degree program. I'd guess most of us have complained about certain courses that were required and you perceived that they were not at all relevant to your major, right? The intellectual buffet did offer a sample of many disciplines and for some people, reshaped their career path and academic trajectory. Once you find a business vertical that provides you with career satisfaction, begin focusing, specializing, and promoting yourself in those spaces. Again, using the academic analogy, a master's degree program, in a focused subject matter is akin to this part of your career path. Here we begin to specialize and strive to be experts in our field, masters of our chosen industry.

Organizations can be similar to individuals in that organizations are driven by individuals. It is truly a hypocritical conundrum that I have personally experienced throughout my career where the required disciplines, required experiences, and general expectations are in reality far from aligned by the outwardly recruiter, head-hunter, and job-board proclaimed criteria. The reality is, in some instances, what they say they want may be inaccurate or the whole process is just a rouse to thwart the equal opportunity police.

Obviously you can just wing it, and maybe you'll win, but my advice would be to bolster your chances for success by the reasonable and realistic preparations you can conduct ahead of competing for that leadership position. You will need to be prepared to compensate for your shortcomings and showcase your strengths. I'm not going to discourage you from making an application to a position that you want but do not match the letter of the job description and requirements set by the employer. You automatically lose by not trying and you stand a chance of winning by making the attempt. My suggestion is simply to be realistic about your qualifications. Dedicate your spare time to complementing your war chest with advanced academic degrees or training and industry-recognized certifications that complement the position you desire. For example, when I decided that I wanted to be a chief information security officer I certainly knew that having a bachelor's degree in computer science would most definitely be required. I also knew that as a senior executive who would interface with other executives such as the chief finance officer (CFO) or the general counsel, there would be additional training in business above and beyond technology. For me, the obvious choice was to earn a master's in business administration (MBA), which I did. I can now tell you that in hindsight, this was a very solid approach and it put me on essentially equal operating ground with any of the other executives, and in some cases, it put me academically ahead of the elder executives. Most people seem to drift into complacency in life. Use this to your advantage! I was recently contacted by an executive recruiter concerning another C-level position.

During our lengthy, exploratory discussions on a few occasions, we reviewed credentials required and experiences desired by this employer as well as other more esoteric discussions that related to the company. Shortly following this preliminary interview phase, while another candidate was in a holding pattern waiting for a progress update, I completed my doctoral degree in cyberspace law. I always keep recruiters updated about important elements of my candidacy and of course informed him of my academic status. His response was "Michael, congratulations! You are a weapon!" That was one of the most amusing and totally appreciated responses and exactly the type of expression you should strive for as well. To be considered a subject-matter expert, the go-to person, the weapon of choice is definitely the lofty status we strive for. Be that weapon!

Interviewing

Well, the time has come! It's time to press the suit and shine the shoes. The economy is tough; you have diligently kept your eye on the job market and a potential employer has shown some interest in your credentials. They would like to interview you. Hooray! Executive-level interviews do not come around too often, so now is your chance to demonstrate to this prospective employer that you, above all others, are the right candidate to choose.

This may not sound like a difficult task, but believe me, there are many tricks and traps along the way that will cause you to snatch defeat from the jaws of victory. Employers want to know if you are a visionary leader who can partner with the lines of business, whether you have good customer service skills, if you speak the language of business, and can leverage your responsibilities to drive revenue or potentially create new business opportunities. Gone are the days executives focused solely on core responsibilities. The CIO can no longer hide out in the data center ensuring that technology supports the current organization. Now, that same executive must be technologically savvy, must understand the organization's business objectives, and must progressively develop ways of leveraging technology to eliminate the pain points other executives face, provide business continuity and operational stability, all the while, culturing future growth potential. A similar paradigm shift has occurred for other candidates vying for executive seats. CFOs now need a bit of technical acumen just like CIOs now need a bit of business acumen. Organizations are becoming more tightly integrated and companies are consolidating, which places a greater burden on all members of the executive team.

When an organization is interviewing a potential executive candidate, they are trying to ascertain whether or not you possess some fundamental requirements. One of their goals will be to solve existing business problems they are experiencing. Your job is to identify that pain point, and articulate how you will be able to help them achieve success. They may be interested in understanding what you do to achieve a certain business goal such as mergers or acquisitions, or perhaps turn around a failing initiative. Pay special attention to the questions you are being asked. In many cases, there will be clues, if not outright direct questions, which you will need to draw upon using your history and articulate how and why you will succeed where others potentially have failed or struggled. Companies look for certain key competencies and characteristics such as leadership ability, strategic thinking, business acumen, relationship building, and, of course, the ability to successfully get the job done. This initial stage may also be a cursory exploration of whether or not you would be a good personality match with the rest of the leadership team. You must understand that every question you're asked has a purpose. Your goal, should you choose to accept it, is to prove that you're the best candidate for the job.

Executive interviews are quite different to those you encounter earlier in your career prior to competing for that executive position. First off, be prepared for approximately three to five separate interviews. It is important to be patient although this is a very difficult thing to do, especially for those of us who have trouble sitting still. You may really need or really want the position but being overly persistent will not help your chances and may actually harm them. Remember, the people interviewing you at this time don't know you or your personality and it is the wrong time to attempt to make "best friends" or socially network or demonstrate desperation.

The very first round of interviews is typically designed to weed out the candidate pool. Many companies will take what typically is an enormous candidate list and attempt to thin the list to less than four to five candidates. Typically, a senior representative from human resources will work directly with the hiring manager and maybe other key internal business partners first to assemble a few basic questions as well as ascertain the hiring manager's preferences. The human resources representative will most likely be not at all skilled at what you are interviewing for, so avoid technical deep dives or other deep discussions if possible. Your initial objective is to be among the first three to five potential candidates for subsequent rounds of interviews with other individuals or groups.

I've mentioned this before, but it is worth stressing again due to the phase of employment you are in at this point. Again, a word of caution concerning the first round of interviews is the typical question that human resources will always ask, and again, that is, "What is your current base salary?" I can't imagine anyone being happy about answering that question. It is a question that is designed to lower the cost of employee ownership so to speak. It is a question that encourages you to lie, knowing that it is a question designed to lower your base salary. My very best advice in dealing with this question is to first, as I've mentioned before, research the current market conditions and salary surveys that are widely available in an effort to develop some reasonable expectations for salary and other compensation so that you will have reasonable expectations from your potential employer. Keep in mind that one of the major differences between compensation for a corporate employee who is not an executive and the corporate employee who is an executive is huge. For example, the only compensation for a regular corporate employee is probably just a base salary. On the other side of the corporate employee spectrum, an executive's compensation starts with a base salary that is obviously more significant. Add in a bonus structure, which is as variable as the imagination can envision. Executives typically get relocation expenses and arrangements completely coordinated by professionals. Executives usually get other perks like house hunting travel expenses, lump-sum sign on payments, stock grants, and other forms, depending on what the company does.

A second thing I would suggest concerning answering this imminent question is, once you are armed with the knowledge you have extracted from current salary surveys, decide for yourself, what is the minimum base salary you would be satisfied with, and answer that question with a simple statement. For example, "The minimum starting base salary that I will accept for this position is $175,000." There are only two possible outcomes, one of which will occur should you answer their question as I have suggested, and that is, "I'm sorry, but that salary is much more than we are willing to pay." At this point, it is prudent to withdraw from the interview process or negotiate an alternative. Accepting a position that does not meet or satisfy your personal financial needs will only bring about job dissatisfaction and that rarely ends well. The second possibility is that the minimum base salary requirements you state are perfectly acceptable and the company understands your needs. Ambiguity is neither your friend nor is it the friend of your potential employer. Your job satisfaction level will be so much better when you achieve your goals, which include financial ones, and you can focus on occupational success.

The next interviewing rounds will most likely be directly with the hiring manager and maybe with other interviewers who will be affected by your appointment. You should expect to have discussions that are more tactical and strategic in nature and you should be prepared to discuss how your experience will facilitate your success. Be prepared, and come into this interview armed with the facts that you collected during your first interview, from the actual job description, and other sources of credible information you may find that will help you understand what challenges the company faces. You need to look beyond just the SEC filings, the financial analyst reports, or financial statements. Understand that this stage in the interview process will be more conversational in nature so it is vitally important to be well-prepared so that you can converse with ease. This interview will most likely be more of a free-flowing, candid event. The focus will most likely be focused on what the company's challenges are and how you will make a difference. Something to keep in mind is to make an attempt at ascertaining why or how your predecessor succeeded or failed. You will need to ask probing questions that will impress most interviewers. You may uncover issues or other cultural impediments you might face as a candidate that of course gives you an advantage over the competition. You want to demonstrate that you have a sincere interest in the company and that you are intellectually curious, both of which are important assets to any executive.

It would be wise for you, prior to your interviews, to search for current or even former employees who would be willing to share some of the challenges the company faces, the corporate culture, or even opportunities they perceive existing. Your social networks will be fertile ground for this activity. Rest assured, your future employer will be searching the social networks and other sources for information about you, so do the same for them. Like I always say, you never know when you're auditioning, so be careful not to make a fool of yourself or later regret the words you speak or type.

Now I would like to touch on using technology during your interview. First off, disable all sounds and vibrations your personal communicating devices make while you are interviewing. They are distracting to everyone and it is rude to interrupt your interviewer. While waiting to begin the interview, you may be tempted to use your phone and I would discourage this. You cannot be certain who is watching or listening and don't assume that the hiring manager's secretary is not important to your success. Should that person overhear an unflattering conversation, rest assured that it will get back to the hiring manager and potentially cost you the position. The second technological point I'd like to make is that discreetly recording each interview is a great way to learn from the experience. Should you have subsequent rounds of interviews, you will be able to the interview and take notes or otherwise prepare for subsequent rounds of interviews with extraordinary accuracy. For those of you who might be questioning the legality of covertly recording your interviews, I'll address that specifically later on, but searching for federal and state eavesdropping laws will provide you with the specifics for your location.

The next big round for you will most likely include a larger group of executives and other senior members of the organization. You can expect these interviews to be less tactical in nature and to be more relationship based. Remember what you learned from earlier interviews about the company's pain points or challenges and other initiatives that were discussed. Those prior discussions will most likely be interwoven into the current interview. The difference being, rather than more technologically focused, your answers will need to be centered on how you build relationships and create partnerships. It will be a good opportunity to discover, through direct and candid questions, what challenges these other executives face and it is appropriate to tell them, based upon your previous experiences, how you can help them be more effective or how you might eliminate those challenges for them. These executives will most likely freely discuss what they see as significant or unexplored opportunities for the company and they will no doubt have an opinion of why the organization is not there yet. This is of course another opportunity for you to dovetail your previous experiences. During your interview, you may start to identify certain themes, opportunities, or challenges, and, of course, draw upon your own experiences and skills, looking for ways to speak about them.

Your final round of interviews at the executive level will most likely be with the CEO and potentially with board members. This will not be the case, generally speaking, for certain executive level positions such as chief information security officer or chief technical officer, but you can pretty much expect it for all other executive level positions. If your final interview includes meeting with the chief executive officer or board members, you'll make a mistake if you focus on technical details and completely miss strategic ones. The CEO will be more interested in your strategic thinking abilities at that moment. Should you have a segue to do so, ask questions about things that are important to the board or that are important to the CEO that will help you speak to those challenges and issues, drawing once again from your experience and skill set. The good news is, if you have made it this far, meeting with the CEO or even another executive at will be your boss, you have already successfully made it past all the other interview challenges and this phase will most likely include an offer for employment. Now is not the time to relax. Now is the time to stay focused and on point.

Whether you choose to accept or reject a job offer, you must inform the employer who made that offer. This should be done formally, in writing, and if you wish, by telephone as well. If your answer is yes, it's obvious why you'll want to make a good impression with your future employer. But, why is it important to be polite to someone you don't plan to work for? Well, you don't know where your future will take you. You may at some point wind up with that employer as a superior, a colleague, a client, or even your next door neighbor. You certainly don't want to leave a bad impression.

It is important to remember, that while you may have now been offered the position you worked so hard for, not to let your guard up or think that the interviewing process is completely over. Until you sign contracts of employment, background checks are completed, and you are actually on the job working and receiving compensation, that employment offer may be rescinded at any time for any reason. So you have an occasion to visit socially for dinner or other meet and greets, consider yourself still vulnerable and that this may be a continuation of the interview process. Be wary of social networks and disclosing any information. It may be perfectly benign, or you may say something that you later regret, so it is best to avoid any exposure until your employment is secure. Remember, you never know when you're auditioning!

Correct interpretations

"All things are subject to interpretation whichever interpretation prevails at a given time is a function of power and not truth." - Friedrich Nietzsche

Most of us are keenly aware of how interpersonal communications can be a real challenge sometimes, even most of the time. A word of interviewing caution is appropriate right now in light of the discussion above. There are a few basic communications principles that are well-established and worthy of discussion and might very well be the point of delineation between success and failure. You certainly would not want to stumble during that important interview would you? These principles underline the workings of real life interpersonal communications. They are fundamental to communication and we should not ignore them.

The first principle is that **interpersonal communication is inescapable.** We can't avoid communicating. The very attempt not to communicate does in fact, communicate something. We communicate not only through words, but through tone of voice and through gesture, posture, facial expressions, and so forth. We constantly communicate to those around us, which is why I am bringing this subject up. Through these various communication channels, we constantly receive communication from others and people judge you by your behavior, not your intent.

The second principle is that **interpersonal communication is irreversible** which means that you can't really take back something once it has been said. The effect must inevitably remain. Despite the instructions from a judge to a jury to "disregard that last statement the witness made," the lawyer knows that it can't help but make an impression on the jury. There is a Russian proverb that I am fond of that says, "Once a word goes out of your mouth, you can never swallow it again." I'll elaborate more on the subject in part two of this book.

The third principle worth discussing is that **interpersonal communication is complicated.** No form of communication is simple. Because of the number of variables involved, even simple conversations are extremely complex. Whenever we communicate, there are really at least the essence of six "people" involved: 1) who you think you are; 2) who you think the other person is; 3) who you think the other person thinks you are; 4) who the other person thinks he or she is; 5) who the other person thinks you are; and 6) who the other person thinks you think he or she is. Confusing?

We don't actually swap ideas; we swap symbols that stand for ideas. This also complicates communication. Words (symbols) do not have inherent meaning; we simply use them in certain ways, and no two people use the same word exactly the same.

There are a few communication maxims that I've heard over the years and I trust you will find them amusing as well.

- If communication can fail, it will.
- If a message can be understood in different ways, it will be understood in just that way which does the most harm.
- There is always somebody who knows better than you what you meant by your message.
- The more communication there is, the more difficult it is for communication to succeed.

These tongue-in-cheek maxims are not real principles; they simply and humorously remind us of the difficulty of accurate communication.

Finally, **interpersonal communication is contextual**. In other words, communication does not happen in isolation. It is comprised of many distinct nuances worth exploring. For example, there is the **psychological context**, which is who you are and what you bring to the interaction. Your needs, desires, values, personality, and so on all form the psychological context. Keep in mind that the you referred to above represents both participants in the exchange or interaction.

There is the **relational context** that concerns your reactions to the other person in the particular exchange or interaction. The **situational context** deals with the psycho-social *where* you are communicating. For example, an interaction that takes place in a boardroom will be completely different from an interaction that takes place in a social networking environment. Speaking of environment, the **environmental context** deals with the physical *where* you are communicating. Physical location, furniture, acoustics, noise level, temperature, season, and time of day all are examples of factors in the environmental context.

Finally, there is the **cultural context** that includes all the learned behaviors and rules that affect the interaction. If you come from a culture where it is considered rude to make long, direct eye contact, you will, out of politeness, avoid eye contact. If the other person comes from a culture where long, direct eye contact signals trustworthiness, then we have in the cultural context a basis for misunderstanding.

Work life balance

A subject that I will discuss in detail as it pertains to corporate culture is work-life balance This is a crucial element of your employment, whether you recognize it or not. Work-life balance is a broad concept encompassing the proper prioritizing between *work* (career and ambition) on one hand and *life* (pleasure, leisure, family, and other personal development) on the other. Another related, broader subject to aware of is that of lifestyle balance. Each of us have interests and responsibilities outside of the work environment, right? Because we all have different needs, aspirations, and motivators, it is only logical that the balance we desire to affect this mixture should be a topic of discussion during your interviews. It is a subject I will explore with you in more detail when we get to the corporate culture segment of this book. From a more generic standpoint, many corporations in today's economy want to better retain and utilize the potential of all professionals, including females, males, minorities, and so forth. In progressive corporations today, there are workplace policies that address the work-life balance challenge that can benefit the lives of working parents and the lives of their children and simultaneously promote workplace retention, diversity, productivity, and improve the bottom line. You will be able to get a sense for this by reading the public news bulletins your prospective employer may be featured in. If there are articles about family-friendly-themed topics, you may safely assume that at least the corporation's public face supports a healthy balance. It is still wise to ask some exploratory questions though.

Word on the street indicators, if they are available.

"Say it with roses, say it with mink, say it forever, then say it with hyper-link." – Michael D. Peters

Part of the research you have already accomplished concerned the financial health of a prospective employer. It is also important not to neglect company reputation, or your own for that matter. Getting a feeling for the word on the street about a particular prospective employer is important and most companies in my experience are very concerned about theirs. Make no mistake; potential employers are also looking at you. You may not be aware of this fact until a recruiter calls to discuss a job opportunity. Reputations are vital. In general, a reputation is the social evaluation by one or by many entities toward you the individual, a group of people, or any organization based upon infinite criterion. It is an important factor in many fields, such as education, business, online communities, or social status.

A reputation could be considered an extension component of your identity as defined by others. I would suggest that your reputation is your ubiquitous, spontaneous, and highly-efficient mechanism of social control in natural societies. For example, during an executive-level interview, the interviewer commented that there was plenty of information about me available online; credentials, publications, presentations, resume, business contributions, and an assortment of other work-related elements were easily accessible to the public. He said that everything was meticulously groomed. He then went on to ask what I like to do for fun because there was nothing he found that had a personal element to it. I had to admit it was extremely gratifying to me to hear that. You never know when you are auditioning! It is my intent to publicly showcase my business— employability attributes— and *not* showcase me making a fool of myself at my reunion or flaming someone on *Facebook. com*, for instance.

In general, reputation is a fascinating subject of study into social, management, and technological science spaces. Its influence ranges from competitive settings, like markets, to cooperative ones, like firms, organizations, institutions, and communities. We should consider reputation as a fundamental instrument of social order, based upon distributed, spontaneous, social control. We, after all, don't call it social networking for no good reason. Reputation is a socially-transmitted belief and concerns properties of agents, namely their attitudes toward some socially-desirable behavior, be it cooperation, reciprocity, or norm-compliance. Reputation plays a crucial role in the evolution of these behaviors: reputation transmission allows socially-desirable (or undesirable) behavior to spread. Reputation accounts also for the transmissibility, and therefore, the propagation of reputation.

If you consider for a moment your reputation on the street or a corporation's, there are certain methods of spinning information that might persuade or dissuade you from pursuing an opportunity, and of course, inversely, a prospective employer from pursuing you. Social networks are informal settings for your reputation to live. Formal settings are more authoritative by nature, and may be public records, corporate communications, affiliations, and other sources.

Traditional reputation management requires close attention to how a company or candidate is perceived: narrowing the gap between perception and reality, identifying competitive advantage, and communicating to select audiences. The new twist to managing your street reputation also requires relentless attention to online advocates and adversaries. We need to attend to a diverse and all-powerful portfolio of stakeholders that now include online media, focus groups, bloggers, Twitterers, and citizen journalists that constantly command attention. Armed with little more than a computer and an opinion, some of these chat-room transmitters and bloggers can undo a reputation by disseminating misinformation and innuendo instantly.

The Internet, and more specifically, the social media and mobile media revolution is clearly a double-edged sword. It presents opportunities for, as well as barriers to, building reputation, recovering lost reputation, or boosting a languishing reputation. On the one hand, the Internet allows an unfavorable problem or issue to remain before the public interminably. If harnessed properly, technology has the potential to effectively air important points of view and quickly counter negative perceptions. It affords a candidate or company the opportunity to address a problem before it explodes and prepare stakeholders before any damage is done. Keep in mind that our new communication and research conduits are now always-on and always-open for business.

Online reputation is a factor in any online community where trust is important. It affects a pseudonym rather than a person. To begin developing an online reputation, consider how your personal or company brand should be perceived. What is your brand identity; what is your value proposition; what should be your selling point or unique voice? Once you have developed the image you would like your constituencies, past, present, or more importantly, future, to perceive, develop a strategy to build your brand. Are you seeking credibility in the marketplace? If you are, then consider blogging or answering questions on *LinkedIn.com* industry groups or build a network of contacts in professional or social websites. Your digital footprints accumulate through all of the content shared, feedback provided, and information that is created online. People generally aspire to have a positive online reputation.

So much depends on reputation; guard it with your life. Reputation is the cornerstone of power. Through reputation alone you can intimidate and win; once it slips, you are vulnerable. You should strive to make your reputation unassailable. Just as corporations have reputation officers and agents to control their reputation, so should you try to control your reputational story. Always be alert to potential attacks and thwart them before they happen. There are both legal and public avenues to remedy negative information that is publically available. It just takes time and in some cases, other resources to remedy the situation. I've heard before, that "the higher they are, the harder they fall." This expression seems simplistic to me. Why would this not hold true? After all, the loftier a person soars, the more visibility that person has. Why would anyone notice someone who contributes nothing to society? Why would anyone notice the newcomer? There will always be upstarts nipping at your heels as they make their personal attempt to replace you within the upper echelon.

Get promises in writing.

"Trust but verify." – Ronald Reagan

The most difficult part of your very successful interview is concerned with the employment contract. This document will ultimately make or break your employee experience and will or will not provide effective protections to you. They, like all effective contracts, are written for the benefit of the assignor and not the assignee (this means you). While most employment contracts are generally innocuous, especially in the all-will employment locations, which are essentially everywhere, there are some basic parameters to keep in mind. I use the word innocuous because contracts can be made and contracts can be broken. I could share several instances where my contracts were broken or modified (essentially broken) without my consent or much prior notification. A specific instance that I'll share revolved around the severance package language that all senior employees enjoyed having in their employment contracts. My particular agreement that I negotiated during the interview process afforded me six months of salary in a lump-sum should I be terminated for any reason without fault; pretty comfy, right? This company began to experience difficulties as a direct result of executive fraud and the board of directors moved to eliminate all severance packages for all employees including that of yours truly. Did I have options at that point? Sure I did. I could have waged a private or class action lawsuit against the company. While I'm an employee, this basically amounts to a death sentence and a personal choice you make independently.

My example fortunately is the exception to the rule and most employment contracts are reasonable, albeit slanted toward the employer's favor. Remember, if it is not captured in your contract, it does not exist and will not come to fruition. For example, if your contract stipulates that "moving expenses are reimbursed" and not "moving expenses are paid-for by the company" you will discover that your out-of-pocket expenses for relocation just exploded and you will now have additional stress to contend with. Another element often neglected by employers is severance language. In my experience, the best severance package I negotiated was "in the event of loss of employment, through no personal fault, the employee is paid a lump-sum equal to six months of base salary," and the worst consisted of no severance. Keep in mind that executive employment generally takes about three to five months to secure so even a modest severance package will help you weather an unemployment storm so do your best to include it. Employers will do their best to use guilt or the uneasy subject matter to appease your mind into neglecting severance language, but you can always assure them that in the end, because all is well, it costs nothing to provide this protection to you and goes a long way to making you feel secure.

Part 2

Now that you have arrived.

"Leadership is action, not position."
- Donald H. McGannon

The sweet smell of success! You have worked diligently to cultivate your skills and experiences. The key to your continued success will be determined within the next one-hundred days. This relates to a question I have often been asked in an executive-level interview: "What does your first one-hundred days look like to you?" Be prepared to answer it. After the very big job of finding a new job is complete, it's time to relax, right? Wrong. Your first one-hundred days in a new position are critical, especially when it comes to relationship building. What you do or overlook during this time can color your entire tenure with a company, or even cut it short, if missteps during this period are big enough. First impressions mean everything and believe me when I say to you that all eyes are on you. It very much reminds me of being a kid again after moving to a new town and starting school. Everyone seemed to be interested in what the new kid was going to do. Now is your chance! The true indicator of leadership is in the power of influence, nothing less, and nothing more.

After you have waded through all the forms and orientation materials, you'll most likely want to roll up those French cuffs and jump immediately into the mountain of work that has been waiting for your arrival. While the sentiment is admirable, especially if the managers you interviewed with wanted someone who could "hit the ground running," you'll be doing yourself and your new employer a disservice if you start making moves at the expense of establishing effective relationships. I guarantee that your early groundwork to establish relationships will pay off handsome dividends down the line.

While you're doing all that meeting and greeting, be on the lookout for the go-to people, the ones who know how to get certain jobs done, no matter where those people fit on the organization chart. How do you find these people, you might ask me. While you are making the rounds, try asking some leading questions like, "who do you recommend I speak to now and get to know?" You'll know you've hit on the right person when several new acquaintances answer with the same name(s).

Now that you've identified the go-to people, go to them! You should begin cultivating relationships with those keystone people early on. Some people like informal office meeting while others appreciate lunch meetings. Make it a point to understand the structure of the division in which you work within and set up meetings with the people who you think seem to be setting the tone. This allows you to develop a relationship with them, and you can also do a bit of selling of your talents, interests, and do some positive internal marketing of the organization you just joined.

At first, and depending on what particular position you hold, you may only possess a modest level of influence. There will be inherent influence that is conferred by your new title. The only thing that new title can really buy is a little time to either increase your level of influence with others in the organization or for your level of influence to be undermined by you or your adversaries. The proof of your leadership will be found in the people you lead and influence.

> "The key to successful leadership today is influence, not authority." - Kenneth Blanchard

In this life, I've been exposed to many different leaders. Some of these people were designated, while others emerged over time. In my opinion, it is always an easier task to be the new sheriff in town where others must take time to develop their opinions and impressions about you. An advantage that this affords is that you have the opportunity to culture your skills and effectively start over fresh each time. A few important aspects you should consider if you find yourself in a place of leadership is you must maintain a reasonable amount of insulation between you and the people you intend on leading or even those who you may potentially be in the position to lead. Efficiently dealing with personnel duties without becoming emotionally involved, but projecting empathy, is one facet. A second component to consider is to say less; loose lips sink ships. The more you disclose to others that you lead, the more your credibility and reputation may come into question. I have always been able to count on people talking and disclosing more about themselves than they really should. That is an important tidbit for any leader to remember. Don't fall into the chasm that is your big mouth. Part of this lesson comes with maturity and part of it from a true sense of discretion few possess. True leaders are able to exercise discretion and restraint. A third thing to consider, but certainly not the last, is about give-and-take. You really should avoid being in the position of taking from the people you lead. It might be a personal favor, or it may be material good, or it might be friendship. In doing so, you potentially compromise your professional relationship and cast a shadow on yourself in the eyes of others you lead who may perceive that justice does not prevail in your shop, or favoritism exists, or that they must also attempt to build these pseudo relationships with you as well. This only leads to moral decay and the consumption of valuable productivity we can never have too much of. I'll share more about subordinate dynamics later.

> "A new leader has to be able to change an organization that is dreamless, soulless and visionless ... someone's got to make a wakeup call." - Warren Bennis

You should make every attempt to be regal in your own fashion: you must act like a king to be treated like one. Now I'm not telling you to start pointing your finger and giving orders here but it is something unspoken. In my experience it is very true that the way you carry yourself will often determine how you are treated by others around you. Leaders command respect because it is apparent that they deserve it. In the long run, appearing vulgar or common will make people disrespect you. A leader respects himself and inspires the same sentiment in others. By acting appropriately professional and confident of your leadership powers, you make yourself seem destined for greatness. In my mind, this is all about what we as individuals aspire to. Do I want to be lost in the crowd, or do I want to rise above the fray? People crave a leader, someone who is charismatic and commanding, and someone who is polished and respected. Occasionally, when I send my child off to school or if they set out on life's journey, I will say to them, "Represent your family well." It is another aspect of this that must be considered. We are either elevated or tarnished by the company we keep. I have banished good friends because their personal behavior brought shame through association to me and I cannot tolerate that negative influence. In the end, we have only our self-respect and reputation to contend with.

The relationship you want built on the strongest foundation possible is your relationship with your boss. I'd recommend putting the shoe on the other foot and essentially "interviewing" your manager—on day one, if possible. Find out what makes them tick, why they joined the company in the first place, and, most importantly, what their priorities are, so that these become some of your priorities too.

Perhaps the most important piece of advice for your first one-hundred days is to establish yourself as a team player by doing more listening than speaking. Too many new leaders fall into the trap of trying to prove their worth by offering unsolicited opinions or making odious comparisons to "how we did it at my last job," which typically will not impress anyone. Employers and fellow employees want to know you are on their team now and that you are 100 percent committed. The best way to prove your worth is to be a focused listener to your teammates around you without compromising your integrity or position within the hierarchy. After all, there not too many positions within the organization at this level who technically outrank you, so be mindful of protocol.

It is a perfect time to begin playing on people's need to believe in something and to essentially create a cult-like following. People seem to have an overwhelming desire to believe in something larger than themselves. You can become, in essence, the focal point of such desire by offering them a cause, a mission, a new faith to follow. Always keep your words as vague as possible but certainly full of promise; emphasize enthusiasm over rationality and clear thinking. Part of a team leader's role is to show your new followers the way even if that path is not entirely clear to you at this stage in your employment. Demonstrating confidence and always having the perception of a plan will help establish you as the person other people want to be around and follow into the proverbial battle.

I've been the chief security officer and chief information security officer to several organizations now and my position puts me in the place of enforcer. Generally speaking, in my experience, this is not a role that people cheer about and want to rally around. Instead, what I have experienced is that the majority of people under my "protection" are not at all interested in becoming information security disciples nor do they tend to have the aptitude for it. There is nothing disparaging about that statement; we each are specialists in our own right and it behooves each of us to understand our place in the enterprise, community, tribe, or universe. This effect may work for politicians or public servants, but less so for an information security practitioner. The effect is relevant to the members of a person's team. Continuity and collective cohesiveness is extremely important and applying solid leadership and team player principles lends itself toward the message this suggestion provides to you.

Fundamental Rule 2: Measure Twice, Cut Once

"Human pride is not worthwhile; there is always something lying in wait to take the wind out of it"
- Mark Twain

Lying in wait

As I write this book, a phrase is stuck in my mind; It is "Lying in wait." It's funny how law school has rubbed off on me. Some might suggest that what actually rubbed off is only legal dirt, but I would like to think it is something loftier! The reality is that we are exposed to new ideas along the way. It is inevitable that we are affected by the things we associate ourselves with or participate in. In legal terms, lying in wait indicates a criminal intent premeditated or is evidence of deliberation and intention. I'll borrow the phrase to illustrate something a little less heinous, but nonetheless potentially detrimental to a person's career movement. Now I deliberately said "a person's career" because this scenario works on both sides of the argument. It might be something you institute against an adversary, or it might be entirely directed toward you by a nemesis that is seen or unseen.

You must be aware, and probably already are, that you are surrounded by forces working with you and against you. We would all like to think that coworkers, employers, friends, children, spouses, or other acquaintances will always honor their word or keep their promises and commitments to you but we probably all have experiences where this was not the case, right? Anyone who has been involved in the termination of other employees recognizes the fact that there is no real job security. That people, just like companies, are fickle and subject to getting caught up in hysteria or propaganda or the heat of the moment. For the reason of self-preservation, be mindful to enter into the workplace with your eyes wide open, and with your perception skills turned on. The higher you get within the corporate structure, the more the risks and rewards should become apparent to you. Obviously, since you are reading this book, that rung on the company ladder is an executive spot. You would be wise to be a robust team player, a keen listener and observer of others around you. People tend to disclose their intentions, even by using unspoken conduits. For example, I worked for an organization that the Federal Deposit Insurance Corporation (FDIC) was in the process of seizing because of executive fraud. Part of my role and responsibility involved the preservation of evidence under subpoena. In this particular company, from a hierarchical perspective, my executive position was three levels down from the CEO's position. The fraud that was perpetrated was this same upper echelon. The interesting twist is that because most companies are all based in technology, my role as the chief information security officer gave me control and access to all of this information, or in this situation, the evidence. The senior executive people involved with this caper wanted to abscond with the evidence but lacked the technical prowess to accomplish it. The point that I'll make about lying in wait is that our fate is sometimes determined by other people. If we do not conduct ourselves honorably or with integrity, there may very well be subordinates or other seemingly smaller people around you who have been quietly taking notes, making observations, listening intently, and collecting both figurative and literal evidence to be used against you in a court of law or of public opinion.

Do your best to conceal your intentions and keep people off-balance and in the dark by never revealing the purpose behind your actions if you can help it. If they have no clue what you are up to, they cannot prepare a defense. This was exactly the course of action I took to preserve my honor and integrity while thwarting my enemies who turned out to be part of my reporting structure. By guiding these people far enough down the wrong path, and enveloping them in enough smoke, by the time they realize your intentions, it will be too late. What a tightrope this may be and your personal ambition may be the deciding factor. On the way to your prize, there are people who assist and those who hinder. I think the key is in the silent identification of enemies and allies, to remain agile while carving your own path.

When to lead is as important as what to do and where to go, isn't it? If a leader repeatedly shows poor judgment, even in little things, people start to think that having him or her as the leader is the real mistake. When the right leader and the right timing come together, incredible things happen. This is pretty obvious stuff, right? This is the vote of no confidence scenario. It does make me wonder how that person came into power to begin with. In my observation, this typically occurs though the good-ole-boy network that is frequently self-serving and often fraught with problems. The other mechanism is brute force. When the optimal inspiration-perspiration quotient arrives, there is always someone who answers that call.

Corporate culture

"A company's culture is often buried so deeply inside rituals, assumptions, attitudes, and values that it becomes transparent to an organization's members only when, for some reason, it changes." - Rob Goffee

One of the benefits I've found in being the new kid on the block, or in my profession as a security practitioner, the new sheriff in town, is that you have an opportunity to start fresh. If you are a wise person, you learn from past mistakes or discover refinements that increase your effectiveness and now you have a new opportunity to apply these nuggets to a new organization. A few things I frequently observe and would recommend to, first, never throw the former regime under the proverbial bus. Most people do try to do their best and most people have supporters. A leader can be strong and polite at the same time. It is a rare occasion that I find it necessary to even raise my voice in order to get my point conveyed.

The second nugget is to *look before you leap*. As an outsider, now inside, how can you possibly know what the culture of an organization really is at that juncture? It takes time. Your good intentions to jump right in and fix everything may just get you prematurely uninvited, with or without parting gifts. The third key element I have discovered is that setting reasonably high standards and expectations is a good thing and we must be cognizant of these activities to shepherd them to fruition. Don't be that leader who talks a good game but doesn't live it. You will lose all of your credibility by doing that. Just a few simple preliminary steps up front will foster your rise and acceptance as a leader.

Corporate culture has been defined as "the total sum of the values, customs, traditions and meanings that make a company unique." It should not be something overlooked while you are with a company, looking to join a new company, and especially right after you have joined a new company. I would argue that the higher up in the organizational hierarchy you climb, the more important finding harmony and personal philosophical alignment will be. Corporate culture should be an important factor in your decision to accept or reject a job offer. You must know what values are most important to you, the individual. If you value flexible time away from the office teleworking, a company with a corporate culture that expects late hours and longer working days may not be a great fit for you. If your potential employer's philosophy is a 100% to 0% work-life balance and your philosophy is 60% to 40% work-life balance, then this company isn't a great fit for you. There is an intrinsic value you must consider when making a determination as to what is acceptable to you. If you are able to get an honest assessment from your potential boss beforehand, you may accept this new working paradigm shift, but negotiate a better compensation package to mitigate the extra demands you will be challenged with. I have learned some hard lessons over corporate culture in the span of my career.

A modified example I'll provide to you actually happened to me during an interview with the person who would soon become my new boss, the chief Information officer of a corporation I set my sights on for employment as their first chief security officer. During my lunchtime interview with him, I diligently asked the question, "What is your work-life balance philosophy?" His uncomfortable answer he presented to me in a laughing manner was "My personal work-life balance is 100 percent to 0 percent." Whoa! My mistake was that I did not take him seriously. Not that the prospect of extended working days, evenings, and weekends necessarily would have been a deal killer, I would have just established new expectations and thresholds for myself. My cost-benefit analysis would have changed from a salary based upon a forty-hour work week to an eighty-hour work week, which was the reality of making a deal with that particular devil.

I've heard corporate culture sometimes called "the character and personality of an organization," since it embodies the vision of the company's founders. The values of a corporate culture influence the ethical standards within a corporation, as well as its overall managerial behavior. You will find that some, but probably a minority, of senior management may try to retool or change the incumbent corporate culture. They may wish to impose new values and standards of behavior that specifically reflect the objectives of the organization. As with any change, it may be for better or worse. During my tenure as a corporate executive, I have sampled a wide variety of corporate cultures and they have many personalities that is a direct reflection of their creators. Strong corporate culture is known to exist where employees respond to leadership because they are closely aligned to organizational values. In such environments, strong cultures help organizations operate like fine-tuned mechanisms, moving along with precision, and perhaps only minor adjusting of the existing procedures and processes is required. Conversely, there is weak corporate culture, where there is very little alignment with organizational values. You will find that control must be exercised through extensive procedures and bureaucracy.

Depending on your personality, you might enjoy one particular corporate culture over another. Leadership is what is needed to shape and change corporate culture. Maybe that leadership will come from you? The higher you want to climb up that corporate ladder, the more you need effective leadership skills. The greater and more profound the impact you want to make on those people you come into contact with, the greater your powers of persuasion and influence need to be.

Complain about nothing even if you have something to complain about.

"A man endures misfortune without complaint."
- Franz Schubert

Nobody likes a whiner or complainer in the workplace. Corporations are the same. Almost every workplace has one, the disgruntled employee who frequently complains to supervisors, peers, and subordinates alike. Complaints might range from supervisory style (too demanding, too lenient, or ineffective), workload (too much, too little, or inappropriate), peers (lazy or harassing), salary (always too low), opportunity (too few, too biased), and so forth. Employees such as this typically cause disruptions and dissension in the workplace. This in turn requires an inordinate amount of extra managerial attention.

If you internalize this for a moment, the reality is that there will be disagreements and things that don't really suit your personality or a situation that did not measure up to your expectations. Do your best to suppress an attitude, negative reaction, or some other counter-productive response that puts you on the losing end of the issue. Remember, that managing workplace negativity means not allowing the behavior to continue and, depending on the threshold of the person managing this workplace problem, which might be you, the remedy may be potentially terminal to your career progression.

We all need positive career momentum if we aspire to secure and maintain that executive-level position. It is particularly important for leaders to have their most positive game-face on when interacting with subordinate employees, peers, supervisors, and within the public eye equally. You never know when you are interviewing, right? Left unchecked, that negative attitude may just facilitate an exit interview.

I have experienced situations with my own supervisor that affected my level of job satisfaction as well as my attitude in general. Who has not been in a similar situation at least once in their life? Left unchecked, these negative vignettes fester and erode our effectiveness as leaders. The only outcome to this conundrum is undesirable. Even if your dissatisfaction is warranted, dealing with it ineffectively will only be detrimental to your career progression and reputation. Those two factors are obviously paramount to your success in getting, keeping, or reclaiming that executive title.

For example, during a period of time in my own career, part of my title was as vice president. Many of my peer group within the company had senior vice president in their comparable titles. In my mind, comparing "apples to apples," this represented inequity. I waited until my annual review occurred and raised the question to my supervisor, who verbally acknowledged his recognition and agreement with my point, citing past corporate practices, catching up with current corporate practices as the culprit, and pledged to remedy the inequity in titles. There was no financial benefit to me; it was purely symbolic, which is also important. My supervisor neglected to follow through with his promise to me and the end result was that I developed a resentment towards him that began to erode my overall perception of him. An effective method for me to deal with my disappointment would have been to frame it in a mentally, more healthy way and let it go. Maybe he had a good business reason for not following through? Maybe he changed his mind or maybe he was just a less than effective supervisor? No matter what the reason, the end result is that I should be the one in charge of my attitude, emotions, and destiny, not others. While I will grant the reality that we are all allowed to de disappointed, we also possess the power to keep that disappointment under control. Failure to do so ultimately weighs down our overall effectiveness and personal satisfaction. The best thing you can do is to simply set your own personal expectations. Do this frequently, but only after you have been able to objectively consider all the contributing factors at play; economic conditions, health of the company, your attitude, longevity with the firm, and so forth.

It pays to be tactfully direct when dealing with the people who directly affect and influence your employment. There is no harm in having calm, rational, and perfectly professional discussions with these people to understand their position, potentially clear communication errors, and find some sort of closure and peace of mind for yourself so that it does not become an ongoing distraction for you.

The law in recent years has grown to protect many forms of employee complaints. For example, the law regarding sexual and other forms of harassment requires employers to institute policies that encourage employees to complain if they feel they are being harassed. Likewise, various whistleblower laws protect employees who complain about unsafe working conditions, illegal practices, and the like. These are all examples of legitimate catalysts for you or your coworkers to level complaints against management (which may include you).

Employers are not helpless against chronic complainers, however, although caution is necessary. The best tool for addressing disruptive behavior is a comprehensive code of conduct contained in an employee manual. Rules against insubordination and discourtesy to supervisors, co-workers and customers should be included. Employees who violate these rules should receive a written warning initially and more serious forms of discipline if the misconduct continues. This is not always the case for employees; including senior executives. As long as there are people higher up in your employment hierarchy, these same pitfalls and rules apply to you.

From a leadership perspective, whiners and complainers should be dealt with promptly and decisively. When the complaints interfere with productivity or employee morale they should be addressed. When the complaining involves misconduct or disruption and is not protected, it should be the subject of discipline. If it continues, termination of the disgruntled employee may be the only way to prevent the dissension and malaise from spreading throughout the workforce. An example I might offer is one that I was directly involved with and it concerned a much more junior employee of the company. I was the brand new chief information security officer for a large financial entity. I had the occasion early on to participate in some corporate technical governance meetings in a leadership capacity. There was one employee who was conversationally overly aggressive and combative with anyone, including me. This behavior persisted even when his own manager discreetly signaled him to stand down. While this negative conduct is not appropriate in general with peers, it is significantly more inappropriate when aimed at senior personnel. We cannot have order and professionalism without common courtesy and it takes only one bad apple to spoil the bunch. This employee was a chronic complainer and I realized very quickly that he was a negative influence on the overall team effectiveness, but he also demonstrated a lack of professional respect to me. He became my pet project. He drew undesirable attention to himself that in short order cost him his job and his termination, which I led, served as a visible deterrent to all other employees. Everyone understood that I supported positive contributions and eradicated negative ones.

Communication style

"I have no scenes to help me, and no words are written for me to say. There is no back-cloth to increase the illusion. There is no curtain. But out of the vivid, living dream of somebody else's life I have to create an atmosphere—for that is advocacy." - Sir Edward Marshall Hall

Good communication skills require a high level of self-awareness. Understanding your own personal style of communicating will go a long way toward helping you to create good and lasting impressions on others. It will also help you to develop an understanding of other's communication styles that will facilitate compensating or compatible communicating responses. By becoming more aware of how others perceive you, you can adapt more readily to their styles of communicating. This does not mean you have to be a shape-shifter, changing with every personality you encounter. What I am suggesting instead is that you can make another person more comfortable with you by selecting and emphasizing certain behaviors that fit within your personality and resonate with another.

Communicating effectively is a real challenge for everyone. There are so many unique attributes each and every one of us possess that shapes our disposition, opinion, choices, and affects exchanges. When we communicate with others, it seems to me that if we could just paint a mental picture, it would say a thousand words more effectively than we, the brutes who spew loft piffle. Some common elements that should never be overlooked when attempting to sway favor with the mob would be setting at a particular time and a particular place, add a bit of humanity to encourage sympathy, add in some familiar component of reality that others listening will identify with. Use simple, disarming language to speak to every member of your audience. Try to use a wee bit of visual language to help your audience form the mind's-eye picture you want them to fixate inside their brains. Weave into your conveyance the importance of the event, the magnitude or importance they must realize and agree to in principle. Finally, you must avoid using argumentative characterizations in an attempt to persuade your listeners. The mob is fickle and their attention wanes quickly. If you give them something to remember like that visual image to fixate upon, your point will last longer than just fear mongering alone. There are many ways to discover your own personal communication style which include readily available self-assessment tools and more formal methods including personality tests such as the Myers-Briggs Type Indicator® (MBTI®).

There are three recognized communication styles that I will briefly explore with you, and I'll share some personal experiences along the way. They are the direct, the indirect, and the aggressive communication styles.

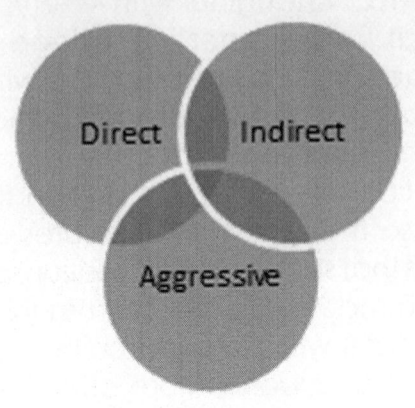

Direct (Assertive)

"But behavior in the human being is sometimes a defense, a way of concealing motives and thoughts, as language can be a way of hiding your thoughts and preventing communication." - Abraham Maslow

This is a style of communicating that I strive for and you should as well. Use it as your primary mode of interaction with others. Users of this communication style tend to be effective, active listeners; they openly state boundaries or declare limits and clear expectations; they will openly share observations, without labels or judgments; they express themselves directly, honestly, and as soon as possible about mixing in personal feelings, emotions and desires; and they help others to keep their feelings and emotions in check as well.

Drawing from personal experience, I can say that keeping perspective on business objectives takes work. We are emotional beings by nature from the start. Over time, as we mature and some develop leadership skills, we begin to master those emotions and start to eradicate them from the leadership equation. A minority segment of the leader's population is able to perceive the bigger picture. They able to see beyond themselves and make decisions that are based on the greater good for the many rather than for the one. When we are able to integrate this higher level of leadership ability into our personal leadership style, our lives are enhanced and our leadership quotients exponentially increase.

Leaders in your position who are effective will always appear to operate deliberately. You must know what needs to be accomplished and you will put together a plan to execute. Action-oriented leaders are fundamental to a successful organization and it is an essential part of your career success. I would recommend you begin improving in this area by looking before you leap. Try to expeditiously understand the challenge at hand and quickly put a plan of action in motion. You must be resolute with your team so you are not perceived as a weak leader, one who flip-flops without a leadership spine. You must be fair and realistic with the expectations and orders you provide the people you lead. It is perfectly acceptable to push your subordinates or team members towards greatness. You are the shepherd to your flock and their success or failure will be attributed to your personal competency or conversely, incompetency; so balance wisely. You actions are supported by your communication style so it's best not to send confusing messages.

Indirect (Passive)

"One secret of leadership is that the mind of a leader never turns off. Leaders, even when they are sightseers or spectators, are active; not passive observers."
- James Humes

I consider the indirect style of communicating to be the most interesting. The reason I say this is because there is enormous utility in the passive, more indirect style of communicating. I have used this style extensively when developing young leaders, allowing them the platform to stretch their wings a bit in a controlled mentoring environment. Clever leaders also leverage this style to indirectly influence others. In a more Machiavellian sense, it is like the marionette pulling strings. The more the scope of your influence expands, the more your power of suggestion will help shape the direction and opinion of the organization you work within.

Passiveness also has its critical applications such as when the issue at hand is minor; when the problems caused by the conflict are greater than the conflict itself; when emotions are running high and it makes sense to take a break in order to calm down and regain perspective; when your power is much lower than the other party's; and when the other's position is impossible to change for all practical purposes (i.e., law, policies, etc.).

There are of course the negative attributes to indirectly communicating. Leaders who by nature communicate passively will quickly develop a reputation of being weak or negative and this repels followers and fans alike. Their indecisiveness or avoidance of conflict and general leadership will quickly be their undoing.

Remaining aware of your own communication style and fine-tuning it as time goes by gives you the best chance of success in business and in life. Your executive tenure will be short lived if you cannot communicate effectively with other people around you.

Aggressive

"The basic difference between being assertive and being aggressive is how our words and behavior affect the rights and well-being of others." - Sharon Anthony Bower

Clearly the assertive style is the one to strive for. Keep in mind that very few people are all one or another style all the time. In fact, the aggressive style is essential at certain times such as when a decision has to be made quickly; during emergencies; when you know you're right and that fact is crucial; and stimulating creativity by designing competitions destined for use in training or to increase productivity. These are all positive attributes that adopting a controlled and manicured aggressive communication style will benefit you in your leadership endeavors.

If you recall the vignette I presented earlier concerning the employee I terminated for insubordination, inappropriate conduct, and other policy violations, his communication style would be considered aggressive and obviously counterproductive to his employment and reputational prosperity.

Everything is ultimately judged by its appearance; what is unseen counts for nothing. Never let yourself get lost in the crowd of averages or be buried in oblivion. I recommend that you do your best to stand out. Be conspicuous almost to a fault and make yourself a magnet of attention by appearing larger, more colorful, and more mysterious than the bland, timid, and mundane masses that surround you. Turmoil can be your friend. Anarchy might be your friend. As an agent of change, I believe it is valuable to realize opportunities that present themselves within disruption, change, anxiety, catastrophe, or other vignettes of evolution. An occasion that comes to mind is an event that would be considered a business catastrophe. The line of business was down for an extended period of time due to a critical service outage. There were employees scrambling to fix a problem that they had no control over and no hope of remedying themselves. The keystone people were working on the problem and everyone else was on standby while we rode out the proverbial storm. That period of anarchy was amusing as I witnessed the masses trying to look busy and appear like contributors to a swift resolution. I recall looking my boss in the eye and telling him that this was the perfect opportunity for my team to implement a significant technical change to the infrastructure without disrupting the business that was obviously, at that moment, disrupted! He agreed and my leadership skills coupled with a situational shift to an aggressive communication style catapulted my project into fruition ahead of schedule. This saved money and resources all the while making me look like the hero.

Mountains are more easily moved with explosives than with a shovel. Sometimes it is the agitator or catalyst that moves us forward. Some of us are perfectly comfortable with anarchy, change, agitation, challenges, and with bludgeoning our way to victory. One man's revolutionary is another man's terrorist, purely by miniscule degrees of separation.

Leadership style

"Management is doing things right; leadership is doing the right things." - Peter Drucker

I'm always interested in the individual philosophy of other leaders in my general pursuit of personal refinement, development, and diversification. One thing that I've learned over the years is that knowledge must be set free, not hoarded by the minority, but shared by the majority. Can you imagine, if over the millenniums, if cultural knowledge had never been destroyed by some invading force? How much further along would we be as a collective species if this practice by the ignorant, invasive, and occupying troglodytes never occurred? One of the great pleasures I take with technological advancement is the notion that information is now nearing the point of immortality. Proliferation preserves and enlightens.

In time, you will discover that your leadership ability will determine the level of effectiveness you will ultimately achieve in your career.. The higher up the corporate ladder you want to climb, the more you need leadership. The greater the impact you want to make, the greater your influence needs to be. Your individual effectiveness and organizational effectiveness is proportionate to the strength of your leadership prowess. The true measure of leadership is influence, nothing more, nothing less. If you don't have influence, you will never be able to lead others. The only thing a freshly-earned executive title can buy you is a little time, either to increase your level of influence with others or for others to undermine your influence. The ultimate proof of effective leadership is found in the followers.

In this life, I've been exposed to many different leaders. Some of these people were designated, while others emerged over time. In my opinion, it is always an easier task to be the new sheriff in town where others must take time to develop their opinions and impressions of you. An advantage that this affords is that you have the opportunity to culture your skills and effectively start over fresh each time. An important aspect you should consider includes maintaining a reasonable amount of insulation between you and the people you intend on leading, or even those who you may potentially be in the position to lead. Dealing with personnel duties efficiently, with empathy, and without becoming emotionally involved is one facet of effective and influential leadership. Another component to consider is that victorious leaders possess an unwillingness to accept defeat. The alternative to winning is totally unacceptable to successful leaders. The way that you may take your victory may not be the straightest path, but one that requires brute force or pseudo-submission. Look for opportunities to transform weaknesses into strength. You might be outgunned and yet your ego compels you to fight on which would be foolish. Take the time to regroup once you have gained better knowledge of your adversary. Careful reexamination sometimes affords you time to strike again, only this time with precision. When the pressure is on, great leaders are at their best. Whatever is inside them comes to the surface. The team doesn't win a championship while its players work from different playbooks, right?

I believe that my personal mantra sums up the essence of this perfectly; "I will bludgeon my way to victory." It is incredibly scary to witness what happens to people in general who suddenly become faced with larger-than-normal challenges. If you were to examine these situations, many of which are captured in the media, you would see anarchy and lawlessness emerge within days of a catastrophe occurring. I have seen people's behavior devolve during Black Friday when the last remaining must-have item sits between possessed shoppers. The one element that maintains order, provides security, and reduces anarchy comes in a form of strong leadership. And I'm not referring to anyone's invisible friend either; I am referring to tangible, flesh and blood leadership.

It is true that the events that occurred in the past do not teach us everything we need to know for the future. I think that it is important to collect evidence of actions and corresponding reactions that have occurred. Knowledge of the past is very much like a tool chest where, at your disposal, is an endless combination of solutions to a current problem. If you could not draw upon the tools you already possess, solving future problems becomes exponentially more difficult.

I've mentioned many times my personal career-progression plan. The same mechanism that makes one work may be equally valuable in planning life's journey. You should have an idea of what sort of person you want to become down the road. You should establish some important goals to strive for, to reach for, and to commit to. As that road winds through life, so should your plan and expectations bend and flow also. Engage your mentors, supporters, and most valuable resources in the process because we are social creatures, dependent on our ecosystem, our community. Be patient but not complacent in life. Engage life with determination. Gold nuggets do not fall from the sky and nothing is preordained. We make our opportunities in this life. Accept the fact that adversity, obstacles, and challenges will be everywhere. Some you may be perceptive enough to avoid, but many will challenge you fully. Remember your successes and accomplishments. They will give you resolution and encouragement. Refresh your life plan or your career plan frequently. This will help you stay focused so you can navigate a more direct path to your goal or your Point B.

Leaders evaluate everything with a leadership bias. People are generally intuitive in their own area of strength and expertise. Who you are dictates what you see. Natural ability and learned skills create an informed intuition that makes leadership issues jump out at leaders. Leaders who want to succeed maximize every asset and resource they have for the benefit of their organization. A leader has to read the situation like tea leaves and know instinctively what plan to deploy. Whenever leaders face a problem, they automatically measure it and begin solving it using their leadership intuition.

This is one of my favorite facets of leadership. It also goes way beyond leadership though. On an individual level, we are charged instinctively and socially with the responsibility for improvement. Our species has not marched forward, has not dominated this planet through complacency, but through empowering change. The persistent analogy I've mentioned concerning wolves and sheep remains true. With that in mind, it is incumbent upon leaders to identify these resources possessed by the people they lead, and leverage these talents accordingly.

It is a well-settled fact that there are extremely varied styles of leadership at our disposal. We are not naturally disposed of some styles while others we are adoptable with time, patience, and persistence. Make no mistake, there is a distinct difference between management and leadership and some are not cut out for one or the other. Your personal trials and tribulations will provide indicators along the way to aide you in areas needing attention, training, and experience.

I'll explore these with you right now and provide personal examples. We first have what is described as authoritarian or **autocratic** leadership. Second, we have the participative or **democratic** leadership style. And finally, there is the **delegative** or laissez-faire style.

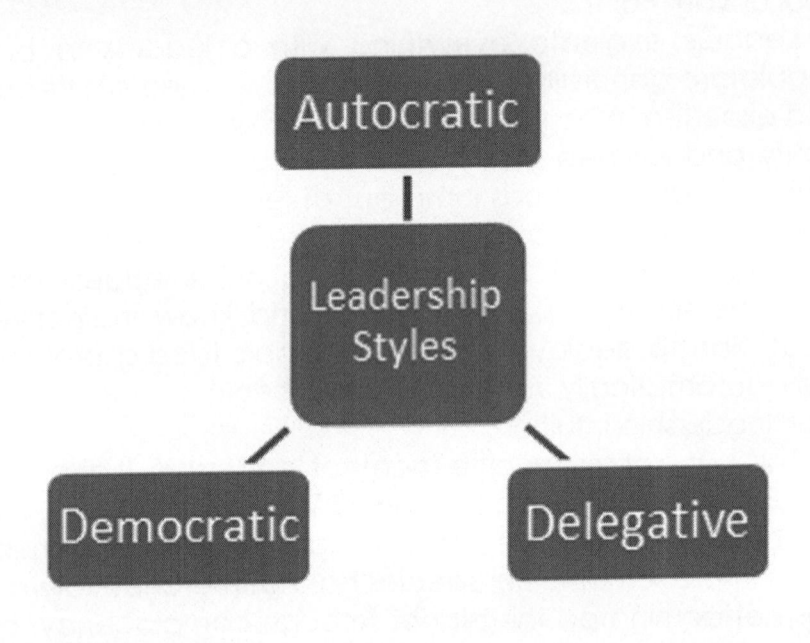

```
        Autocratic
            |
       Leadership
         Styles
        /        \
  Democratic   Delegative
```

Autocratic

"Leaders tell but never teach until they practice what they preach." – Featherstone

Some leaders are more authoritarian in nature. This autocratic style will be more direct by nature. Autocratic leaders tend to exclude most, if not all, outside input in their decisions. They provide clear expectations for the mission at hand of exactly how to achieve the goal. While authoritarian leadership is best applied to situations where there is little time for group decision-making, or where the leader is the most knowledgeable member of the group, the downside is that teams tend to be less creative.

Autocratic leaders get others to do the work for them and always take the credit. They use the wisdom, knowledge, and legwork of other people to further their own cause. Leveraging such anonymous assistance saves you valuable time and energy; it may also give you a superhuman aura of efficiency and speed. In the end your helpers will be forgotten and you will be remembered. You might say, never do yourself what others can do for you. Generally speaking, I don't subscribe too closely with this style of leadership. While I do think that collective accomplishments should be associated with the leader of the group, I also think that if the leader completely usurps the accomplishments of his subordinates, the likelihood of discontent is strengthened. Discontent leads to mutiny. Mutiny results in a power struggle. I've been at both ends of the spectrum and I believe that there is a careful balance that must exist in order to sustain upward mobility, downward contentment, and holistic productivity.

Do not however build a fortress to protect yourself because isolation is dangerous. The workplace is a hazardous place and it becomes more so the higher up the corporate ladder you climb. Remember that everyone has to protect themselves and they all respond to threats in different ways. Dangers and adversaries are everywhere. While building the proverbial fortress around yourself seems like the safest option, isolation actually exposes you to more dangers than it protects you from. Isolation cuts you off from valuable information, making you more conspicuous and an easier target for your adversaries to harm. It is much better, as I mentioned at the beginning of this section, to circulate among people, find allies, and mingle. This will signal to everyone that you are a team player and this will in turn shield you from your enemies. Remember that isolation exudes the appearance of weakness. Don't be caught hiding away like a rodent slinking about with persistent terror. There are far more sheep than wolves in the world. I believe that if a person promotes deterrence, the fear of consequences helps to eliminate potential threats. Never get even, preemptive strikes and escalations are the deterrents.

In my experience in leading people and being led by others at times, I know that the pointing of fingers by leadership only serves negative purposes and provokes the pointing of middle fingers by those who would be led. It is vital to enter the fray with boldness. As a leader, if you are unsure of a course of action at the time, do not go into battle. Your doubts and hesitations will infect your execution and cause your followers to question your leadership. Everyone admires the bold and the brave; no one admires the timid and the weak. I'm not really certain where the expression, "no guts, no glory" came from, but it certainly seems appropriate, wouldn't you agree? I say that confidence comes from a well-conceived plan that becomes a well-executed plan. Subsequent endeavors build on this. There are times when agility and the ability to improvise just gets us through those tight spots, but, I would also suggest that this ability is largely due to the compilation of experiences subconsciously injected into the mix.

Democratic

"Great leaders gain authority by giving it away."
– James Stockdale

Democratic leaders encourage group members to participate, but they retain the final say over the decision-making process. Group members do tend to feel engaged in the process and are more motivated and creative. People do what people see. Great leaders always seem to embody two seemingly disparate qualities. They are both highly visionary and highly practical. The leader's effective modeling of the vision makes it come alive to their followers. Followers may doubt what their leaders say at times, but they usually believe what they do. As we mature as leaders, most of us naturally begin to fulfill the same role as our mentor to others. Even if leaders become disasters in life, the purpose of their existence may very well be to serve as examples to others, and even that serves a meaningful purpose.

As you can imagine, people buy into the leader first, then the vision. The leader finds the dream and then the people. That is true, however, no matter what the leadership style. The people find the leader and then the dream. People don't at first follow worthy causes. They follow worthy leaders who promote causes they can believe in. Every message that people receive is filtered through the messenger who delivers it. As a member of the executive ranks, you will discover this fact to be true. The tempo set by an effective executive leader trickles down throughout the organization to the most entry-level of individuals. People want to follow those they get along with or admire. As a leader, your success is measured by your ability to actually take people where they need to go. But you can do that only if the people first buy into you.

It makes no difference what the objective or the cause, when you have a charismatic person with a mission, that person will inevitably have followers. This principle holds true for democratic societies and suicide bombers alike. If I had any advice, it would simply be to always follow your instincts and not your emotions; attempt to be a better person tomorrow than you were today; and the view is so much better in life when you take the high roads instead of the low.

Delegative

"The best executive is the one who has sense enough to pick good men to do what he wants done, and self-restraint enough to keep from meddling with them while they do it." – Theodore Roosevelt

Delegative leaders tend to offer little or no guidance to group members and leave many decisions up to group members. While this style can be effective in situations where group members are highly qualified in an area of expertise, it often leads to poorly defined roles and a lack of motivation. On the other hand, strong leadership ability promotes empowerment that is a form of delegative leadership.

I think that only secure leaders give power to others. Leading well is not about enriching yourself but more about empowering others on your team to aspire to greatness. The number one enemy of empowerment is the fear of losing what we have. When we suppress or oppress people, we have to go down with them, while conversely, empowering people increases our own power as a leader. Remember, it only requires fear to oppress whereas it takes intelligence, maturity, and skill to effectively become a strong leader.

I certainly believe, through experience, that when we rise up through the ranks, our level of responsibility increases. This level of responsibility should become more strategic and less tactical, necessitating the need for delegation. One of the points of delineation between effective and ineffective leadership comes directly from our power to delegate effectively. Choosing the right partners is a skill that takes time to develop. Instinct, intuition, and common sense are all at play.

Too often we select our friends or those people who agree with us all the time versus those that enrich and challenge us to grow as leaders. Very often, those who ride our coattails fail to appreciate the opportunity we as leaders provide and that unhealthy relationship is most likely going to result in contention. I don't agree that enlarging others makes you larger. This is comparable to social welfare programs that create artificial supporting mechanisms that ultimately result in unhealthy dependencies burdening the sponsor. If we take away the motivation to survive, to strive for something better, to reach for something higher, to encourage complacency, we stifle our own progress. Humans need a good predator. Predators help us stay sharp and progressive.

If you step outside of directly democratic leadership situations, indirect, delegative leadership is something to be kept firmly in mind. Leaders tend to naturally receive more exposure to the general population. As a result, their scope of influence, good or bad, affects others in ways we cannot always predict. With this in mind, it is important to consider your leadership actions carefully and understand that you will influence unknown personalities out there, sometimes with negative, or positive, consequences. I for one strive to be thought of and remembered in the most genuinely positive of ways. As a leader, I recognize that some days I will win, and on some occasions, I cannot.

Peer Group

"You can do what I cannot do. I can do what you cannot do. Together we can do great things." - Mother Teresa.

Look before you leap into a peer group situation. You must choose wisely. Never rush into developing relationships that may become toxic. A leader's ultimate potential is determined by those closest to him or her. The higher up the corporate leadership ladder you climb, the lonelier it gets. It helps to bring even just one trusted associate with you if possible. When you develop your inner circle, take time to gradually assess a candidate's honor, ethics, attitude, and personality. When you get to experience a person over an elongated period of time, it allows for a more in-depth dissection and analysis. You will expose flaws. You will find imperfections. Understanding this composition will provide you with better perspective, better insight, and ideally, a better end result that is based upon intelligent design and not impulse. There are so many deceptive factors such as hormones, stress, fear, levity, and even manipulation influencing our choices. If we can step back for a longer period of time and see firsthand the true colors of those who would be potential candidates for our inner circle, we reap long-term rewards. You should surround yourself with the best staff you can find, develop them as much as you can, and delegate nearly everything you possibly can to them without jeopardizing your own career or reputation.

Once you have made selections, it is time to cultivate those relationships and to encourage potential. Inspiring leaders support other people in their circle of influence and you should consider investing in them emotionally. When you acknowledge their supporting roles or praise people, they flourish; criticize them and they wither or withdraw. Praise and genuine support is the easiest way to connect with people. When people receive genuine praise, their doubts diminish and their spirits are lifted. I imagine we have all experienced this phenomenon during our lives at least once. Encourage people and they'll walk through fire for you. By inspiring those subject to your influence, you will become the kind of person others want to be around. It all starts with mastering the language of motivation, something we just discussed.

Be wary of possible competition

"I have been up against tough competition all my life. I wouldn't know how to get along without it." - Walt Disney

I've been told and I have read that who you are is who you attract or the attention you receive. Who you attract is not determined by what you want but it's determined by who you are. If you think your people, your staff, or your followers are negative, you'd better check your own attitude first. The better leader you are, the better leaders you will attract to your team or support system.

While I support the fundamental, undeniable premise here, I disagree entirely with the notion that success has nothing to do with personal desire. My victory motto, as mentioned before, articulates my personal belief in the power of determination and persistence. We all possess the power to change. Change might come in the form of education, or attitude modification, or in the company we keep, or even in what we define as our Point B in life and then establish our personal marching orders in accomplishing it.

Another aspect that I disagree with is that our human quality attracts the same quality in others who we may lead or who might lead us. Those people who choose to be around us have their own motivations. While I agree that positive attributes attract similar attributes, there are universal attracting and opposing forces at work that we all must face to one degree or another. Instantaneously the relationship between Martin Luther King Junior and James Earl Ray comes to mind, or John Lennon and Mark David Chapman. There are countless examples throughout history that will illustrate my point. For now, I'll stick to bludgeoning my way to victory as honorably as I am able to. I just hope that should I ever attract the attention of a companion comparable to the men I just mentioned, I'll successfully be able to use justifiable self-defense in a court of law.

There are so many questions and variables with this facet. I would certainly do what is necessary in my mind to preserve and protect what I consider most precious and suggest to anyone that they approach it the same way. The notion is such a subjective one. An individual will proclaim their agenda is paramount, while others will declare the same. Who is correct and justified in their position? I think it is more of a question of sheer will, determination, and opportunity. You will discover similarities in your dealings with other people regardless of what level within the organization they hail from. The sad reality is that the more successful you become, the more others will want to compete with your success, at times sparing no expense in doing so. I recall a situation where the corporation was right-sizing and the employee tension could be felt at almost all levels of the organization. You will find that, generally speaking, when you are exempt from these rifts, you are going to be notified of that fact immediately. The people outside that circle are the ones who are oblivious to their fate. I have been fortunate and successful enough not to be on the losing side of that predicament, but it can happen to almost anyone given the right circumstances. There was another executive who I considered a peer. This person was someone who considered himself charming and quite clever. His leadership style was extremely delegative, to a fault I would suggest. During our tenure together, there were times when we each would require input from our respective teams. When I was new to the organization, his support was generally provided with resistance and autocratic bologna. After about a year this changed because he recognized that my power and influence had increased to the point where his light did not shine as brightly as mine, which of course made him unsecure. He decided to form an alliance with me rather than being an obstructionist to my success, a tactic I found to be transparent and desperate. During this whole evolutionary process our professional relationship took, I never relaxed my apprehension towards him because I instinctively knew that he would do his best to usurp my power for his personal gain given the chance. I recall a private lunch meeting that turned into an effort on his part to conjure my support for enlarging his department and his scope of influence. The challenge for him was that this plan directly contradicted the direction our supervisor intended on going. While I listened patiently to his scheming, I held close to the vest my dissention. This plan was thwarted because I supported my manager; regardless of whether or not I agreed with him, it was the reality of the situation and a responsibility as an executive leader to tow the party line. Shortly thereafter, that peer was terminated and I assumed command of his team while retaining my own, effectively doubling the scope of responsibility increasing influence and reach into the corporation, and increasing my power.

Political collaborations, even symbolic ones.

"If you lie down with dogs, you will get up with fleas." – A Proverbs

There may be fierce competition by people who plan to get ahead at any cost. When you decide to join the executive ranks, you will find betrayals, manipulations, deceptions, and exploitations on occasion. We must all form alliances and partnerships as leaders and as executives to survive. There are many ways to accomplish this. These challenges can come from any direction from your peer group to even your boss. The big question is, how do you protect yourself?

I'm not suggesting that the executive landscape is overly riddled with career hazards. I consider the rewards to far outweigh the risks but that is of course a question only you can answer. One thing is certain: you must take charge of yourself, your actions, and you will consequently help yourself avoid many political conflicts or skirmishes. Here are a few suggestions that I have found extremely beneficial in my own executive success.

You have probably heard before, "never let them see you sweat," right? The keystone element there is acting with confident composure at all times. It is a state of mind where you recognize that you can directly command only yourself. You resolve to do so. When you are in charge of yourself, you believe you can better influence the controllable events that take place around you and subsequently act to do so. Before you can lead anyone, you must believe in it passionately and demonstrate it, otherwise you will never gain followers. Inspiring leaders have an abundance of passion for what they do. The bottom line is that you cannot inspire others unless you are inspired yourself. Passion is something that can't be taught. You either have passion for your message or you don't. Once you discover your passion, make sure it's apparent to everyone within your professional circle. You will find recommendations throughout this book that help you to do this. Those followers may be peers or more senior executives right down to the entry-level ranks. Some tactics to help achieve this include expressing your talents and goals through a personal career-progression project plan, as I described in the first section of this book. With a mission, you know where you are going and where you stand. That simplifies life. Your actions become more directed when you do something specifically toward achieving your long-range mission.

You can lose a lot of time trying to figure out what the other guy is doing so stay focused on your own objectives. Although it is helpful to understand your competition, you'll get further and accomplish more by attending to what you can control. When occasional adversaries present themselves, you gain traction by sighting beyond those competitors and by concentrating on your mission while working toward achieving your constructive objectives. Have your heard the expression, "getting lost in the weeds?" This is one aspect that I personally must work harder at. Because my interests and capabilities are diverse, my attention to little things sometimes gets neglected. Don't fall into that trap if you can avoid it.

One of the best ways to avoid the entrapments of distraction is to be organized. This sounds very simple, but in reality it's more difficult than keeping up with your calendar. What I am referring to is your mission plan, the tasks and goals you have distilled out of your known set of responsibilities. You must simplify your own personal system to get the best results with less amount or hassle. For example, before you leave work, create your to-do list for the next day. Emphasize what is most visible and valuable to do and set that as your prime objective. Whenever practical, start with your top priority. Keep your computer or file folders in order to avoid the duplication of efforts and wasting of your time. Work to schedule a fixed amount of time each day to prepare for what comes next. I would always block this time out in my office calendar as *closed door* time. From the outside, others can see that your calendar is not open for meeting at that time. If you do not set boundaries, no one else will respect your time and this will impede your success if you allow others to bring you down in this fashion.

Always do your best to support your ideas with facts and plausible validators if possible. Present your plans and proposals in supportable terms. If you are a legal executive or security executive, which are considered cost centers in business, focus on Annualized Loss Expectancy (ALE) otherwise learn to use the Return on Investment (ROI) formula. Consider what other people are trying to do that fits with your plans and form strategic alliances with them. Whenever feasible, establish conditions for you and others to have a mutual advantage. The benefits are obvious. When asking for help, however, appeal to someone's self-interest, never to their mercy or gratitude. If you need to turn to an ally for help, never remind them of your past assistance and good deeds. They will find a way to ignore you. Instead, uncover something in your request, or in your alliance with them, that will benefit them, and emphasize it out of all proportion. They will respond enthusiastically as they see something to be gained for themselves. This reminds me of my time is spent in college microbiology, where I studied the concept of symbiotic mutualism. Two organisms benefit by collectively working together. To me this concept is very natural. From a leadership and personal power perspective, where appropriate, make other people come to you; use bait if necessary. When you force the other person to act, you are the one in control. It is always better to make your opponent or partner come to you, abandoning his own plans in the process. This is a suggestion to potentially have fun with. Parts of this involve a certain amount of smoke and mirrors. Parts of this involve riding the discombobulating wave. I also think that a portion of this involves managing your own predictability.

Be wary that your increased executive power will present increased levels of public exposure and, depending on your lifestyle, may involve more coffin nails than kudos to you. It is in your interest to project a positive public image. You will want people to think well of you. If you need to establish alliances, you'll have an easier time of it if you do not have what I refer to as "plague boy syndrome," which simply describes a person with a negative reputation who others may avoid like the plague. Working well with others is an extension of confident composure. You'll get further by working cooperatively with people than by butting heads with them. However, you can't win them all. I'd recommend never putting too much trust in friends, peers, and especially family. You should learn how to use your adversaries and enemies. If you are a savvy leader, you would be surprised how well you will be able to leverage indirect leadership skills to orchestrate events for your advantage. Always be wary of co-workers who call you their friend. In my experience, they will betray you more quickly than anyone, especially when you succeed. They will be more easily aroused to envy than a stranger or mere acquaintance. They also tend to become spoiled and tyrannical, believing they have special rights over others. Conversely, try to hire a former adversary or a complete stranger and they will become a more loyal friend, because they have more to prove. You may in fact have more to fear from your friends than your adversaries. This is certainly a situation that I can honestly say I have lived and learned from. Going forward, my management rule will be to never hire friends or family.

Some of us are optimistic and positive by nature while others of us are pessimistic and negative by nature. While there are benefits to a healthy balance within the workplace, too much negativity is the proverbial apple that can spoil the bunch. In a personal sense, my advice is if you downgrade your abilities by comparatively elevating the abilities of others over your own, you end up degrading yourself for not being good enough, a predicament to avoid at all costs. I suggest you build on your strengths and focus on completing short-term goals that dovetail into your bigger strategic plan and relish your accomplishments. Nothing is ever really finished in this life. By being persistent, by bludgeoning your way to victory, your growth and development will eventually serve as an added buffer against workplace politicking.

"Negativity poisons the intellectual and emotional fountain we all drink from." - Michael D. Peters

Get organized quickly

"First comes thought; then organization of that thought, into ideas and plans; then transformation of those plans into reality. The beginning, as you will observe, is in your imagination." - Napoleon Hill

Personal and organizational effectiveness is proportionate to the strength of leadership. It is easy to delay and create excuses for things we fear, are uncomfortable with, lack control over, threaten us, and, in some way, making us insecure. By laying down the groundwork for success now rather than later, you will be able to identify factors you are challenged by and those that you are comfortably proficient in. It's like the headlight to an oncoming train; you see it coming before it hits you.

I am a bit of a visual person and love to create plans, charts, models, flowcharts, and illustrations to use for myself as well as for other's benefit when taking on complex or abstract tasks. For example, before I became an executive, I knew I wanted to be one. I did my homework dissecting the role and trying to understand what it really meant. I collected articles, books like this one, and advice from mentors. From this compilation of knowledge I amassed, I assembled a project plan that included common position criteria functions and in some cases, subtasks. This project plan enabled me to understand the gravity of the task before me and what components I needed to acquire more knowledge, understanding, and skill in.

Consider creating a personal brand

"You cannot kindle a fire in any other heart until it is burning within your own" - Eleanor Doan

Develop a mantra that is used enough that others associate it with you. You might set about promoting a particular expression or ideology that represents your agenda, business plan, or leadership style. A friend and colleague taught me many things about branding. At the time of this writing, he was the vice president of strategy and customer experience for a company we both worked for; I was their chief information security officer. There were many things apparent to me about him. He was energetic, passionate, and knowledgeable about his area of expertise. One of his persistent themes was about brand recognition. He would demonstrate example after example of how commercial retailers help to differentiate and identify themselves to customers, in part, through brand campaigns.

I consider myself a person whose expertise spans a significant number of different subject areas, a renaissance man perhaps. What I heard from him resonated and, naturally, my mind began to take that nugget in many different directions, including what would become my personal brand. I found that I had participated for years in organizations, online publications, traditional publications, television, radio, blogging, authoring, wikis, and whatnot, but nothing really pulled everything together. I thought that my current life's work was rather disconnected. While all of those activities were gaining me recognition as a leader in my field of expertise, real, long-lasting continuity was the missing component. I decided to focus on significant components that made me stand out and distilled a common theme on which to begin the brand recognition task. I started the *Your Personal CXO* network on the popular professional networking site *Linkedin.com*, a site I highly recommend for professional networking. This new brand became a common theme on my personal blog, the Holistic Operational Readiness Security Evaluation HORSE Project Wiki, Technorati.com, and even on my employer's blog.

Work smarter not harder! When I write an article now, I repurpose it on several media outlets; I syndicate the content to a variety of social media sites like Twitter.com, Linkedin.com, Facebook.com, and others to generate buzz about my brand, my efforts. There are a variety of reasons why I decided to engage in these syndication activities. One reason is to get my name in front of as many people as possible because you never know when you are auditioning, right? I have received more job opportunity invitations through sites like Linkedin.com and TheLadders.com that any purpose-built job site. Two, because I will be recognized as an expert in my field; like they say at universities, publish or perish. The way I see it, there are really two reasons for publishing. In part, it is of course for personal gratification and the other is to ideally give back to the practice. It is incumbent upon the generations now to contribute to the generations to come. I don't know about you, but I want to leave a positive and memorable contribution to the world that remains far beyond my last breath.

One thing to remember is that momentum is a leader's best friend. Why is momentum a leader's best friend you ask? Many times momentum is the only thing that makes the difference between losing and winning. Momentum is like a magnifying glass; it makes things look bigger than they really are. Even average people can perform far above average in an organization with great momentum. It takes a leader to create momentum. Leaders always find a way to make things happen. Once you commit to doing something worthwhile, don't let up. I've seen this phenomenon in action and I've applied the principles in real life. The key and the real trick here is to sustain momentum. A leader cannot jump in, pep up the troops, and walk away completely. If the leader does not have a genuine support structure underneath, who will continue the work? Who will sustain that momentum? The average person does not have the ability to maintain clear vision, to persist through adversity, to circumvent obstacles without the support of a commander to provide assurances that many people need to sustain momentum. The key element is the leader. The vision varies. The momentum is only achieved when that particular agenda is adopted by those who will be led and collectively harness that momentum through to fruition. The dark underbelly is that vision. Ignorance has its own leadership hierarchy unfortunately.

Saying less is more.

"A sudden silence in the middle of a conversation suddenly brings us back to essentials: it reveals how dearly we must pay for the invention of speech."
- Emile M. Cioran

Do your best to win through your actions, never through argument if all possible. Any momentary triumph you may think you have been through is really a pyrrhic victory because the resentment and ill will you stir up is stronger and lasts longer than any momentary change of opinion. It is much more powerful to get others to agree with you through your actions, without saying a word. The key here is to demonstrate, not to explicate.

This is certainly a principle I believe in firmly, although the slope can be quite slippery. Our Machiavellian tendencies may ultimately stifle a good plan unless it is properly executed. It is a real asset to possess big-picture vision. If your personal capabilities exceed your adversaries, if you stand taller, your foresight and vision will be stronger. It is very easy to be placed on the defensive by loud and aggressive souls. I have personally weathered many a storm and ambush in my life. I don't mind this too much because I recognize the catalysts behind it such as other agendas, ambitions, stupidity, ignorance, popularity, and so forth. I will admit however that practicing what I am preaching here has been a road fraught with many bumps along the way, some more uncomfortable that others.

With patience and persistence, tides turn and lessons are learned; our success rate will increase. At some point in time, with careful nurturing, our adversaries identify themselves. I'm a patient person. A person who goes into battle cannot expect to remain unscathed, but I do expect to route my enemies. Let the games begin! We will explore this concept more when we examine fundamental rule number three in the next section.

You never appear to be too perfect. Appearing better than others is always dangerous, but most dangerous of all is to appear to have no faults or weaknesses. Envy creates silent enemies. It is smart to occasionally display defects, and admit to harmless vices in order to deflect envy and appear more human and approachable. Only gods and the dead can seem perfect with impunity. I have always considered it a worthy endeavor striving to be that wise sage who only really speaks when there is something truly worth sharing or communicating. Noisy, blathering people only become vexations or distractions to others around them. There is an African proverb that comes to mind: "Speak softly and carry a big stick." I believe a person should be able to exhibit intelligence, wisdom, and consideration without eclipsing those around you unnecessarily by your own illumination.

Part 3

Trouble in Paradise

"To run away from trouble is a form of cowardice and, while it is true that the suicide braves death, he does it not for some noble object but to escape some ill."
- Aristotle

Clash of the Corporate Culture

It happens, the unthinkable, the regrettable situation when your employment takes a turn for the worse. In some cases, the turn can lead to your resignation or termination. I have never believed in this notion of "job security" and question the realistic cognitive faculties of those people who claim to possess it. It may or may not be your fault. The point is that unfortunate events occur, and how are you prepared to manage the situation?

There may be a multitude of reasons for employment adversity: something you did or did not do, something another person has done to you, or even something completely unforeseen and out of your control. In my career, I have experienced, in some fashion, every example that I have provided already. Do your best to know who you're dealing with and try not to offend the wrong person. There are many different kinds of people in the world, and you can never assume that everyone will react to your strategies in the same way. Deceive or outmaneuver some people and they will spend the rest of their lives seeking revenge. They are the proverbial wolves in lambs' clothing. I have reflected upon this scenario many times in my life, particularly while driving a vehicle. I know the intent is really geared towards interpersonal relationships with the people you deal with at work, at play, and at home. However, I cannot help to think about commuters. You never really know, generally speaking, who is in that other vehicle that you are waging a vehicular combat against. I'll offer this amusing analogy to illustration my point. The lack of basic consideration for others and this concept of road rage always amazes me. You just never know who the other person is in that other vehicle; that person could even be an assassin who has just decided, based upon your behavior, that it is pro bono day.

The "Sucker Punch."

"Whenever a man has cast a longing eye on offices, a rottenness begins in his conduct."
- Thomas Jefferson

It is advantageous to be well-connected. Having a network of hunters and gatherers who work for you would certainly be a luxury. The rub would be whether or not you could ultimately trust those worker bees. The conundrum would be, "There is no honor among thieves," perhaps? I do believe that the weakest link in my caper is the other person. I've made quite a career within the information security space and it is a frequent requirement to profile, investigate, pursue, collect, and prosecute, which lends itself to validating my point.

At one point in my career progression, I thought it would be perfectly acceptable to discuss with my immediate supervisor my desire to at some point in the future, succeed the post they command. The following sanitized example took place during my more junior executive tenure with a large international corporation. My supervisor had been with the company for two dozen years, working up from an entry-level programmer to the chief information officer position. He had only his experience with the same company and a bachelor's degree to show for his twenty-four years. In contrast, my experience was with a variety of companies, a bachelor's degree, an MBA in IT Management, and a variety of professional certifications. And if that was not enough, I was also a law school student. My mistake was expressing to my boss during a career development discussion, that I would like his job someday.

While I personally believe that succession planning within the executive ranks, and at most levels, is the prudent thing to do, I discovered some hazards along the way that you need to be aware of. No matter what the set of circumstances are, never tell your supervisor you would be interested in their current position. I could have answered his questioning in a way less threatening, such as, "Someday, when I have earned it, I would like to become a CIO too." My mobility within that company was halted with a singular sucker punch by an insecure supervisor.

From your boss

You should never outshine your supervisor. Always try to make those above you feel comfortably superior, even if you do not consider them to be so. If you do actually desire to impress them, do not go too far in displaying your talents or you might accomplish just the opposite, which is to inspire fear and insecurity in them. It is always prudent to make your managers or leaders appear more brilliant than they are. This point I am making has actually truly been a conundrum, an occasional burden, a point of frustration, along the way for me and I suspect for you as well. Obviously, since you are reading this book, you have similar ambitions. It is most unfortunate that some feel the necessity to conceal their personal talent, zealousness, desire to accomplish great things, and to contribute in a positive way, all for the sake of observing this unspoken rule. On your way to the top, life will seem to be a series of chess moves, always maneuvering, always moving, and leveraging opportunity on your way to the prize.

Under no circumstance should you ever disclose your desire to replace your boss. Keep those saucer eyes to yourself! Everyone will naturally assume that at some point in time, your boss will move up or on and that you would make a potential candidate. If you are a person who has refined your personal career-progression project plan and appropriately cultivated those keystone credentials during your career, excellent, however, be wary that your boss may not have. Your formal education may be stronger, your industry certifications may be more relevant and current, and this may not be the situation for your boss.

I am always amazed at how underprepared so many people are. I'll not get into the weeds holistically, only vocationally. If members of our species did not take chances, explore opportunities, develop tools, and persistently move forward, we would be extinct or dominated by another more capable species. This condition will create an uncomfortable insecurity in those who are reminded of their complacency and inadequacy. This revelation may cause people to react in a manner that is detrimental to their career or current position. People sometimes make decisions that are self-serving, so avoid the pitfall altogether by keeping your career objectives closely guarded. Due to the fact that I have cultivated my personal career-progression project plan as I have recommended to you, I am not concerned with losing my credential edge. I have maintained my formal education and my professional certifications over the years that continue to add value to the overall package I provide to an employer. I encourage you to do the same.

From a peer or co-worker

Unless you live and work in Utopia, workplace sabotage from a peer, or anyone for that matter, should not be an issue in your professional environment, but sometimes colleagues can be envious, overly competitive, or otherwise motivated for some other reason. Dealing with difficult people is a skill all leaders need to have. In my experience, there are a few tactics you should employ to neutralize the threat that they pose to you.

First, do your best to positively identify the source of sabotage. If you believe that your peer is taking credit for your work or otherwise undermining you, make sure that you confirm that this is actually occurring. It pays to keep an objective perspective on the situation. To do otherwise can be terminal to your career. Sometimes workplace stress can skew perspectives or other external agitators can make the situation appear the way you perceive it, or you might be right on target.

Second, always meticulously document the situation. Make sure that you identify and save out any relevant e-mails and documentation that verify that your point of view is accurate. Just like law enforcement or secret agents do, keep everything. Your position is sometimes only as good as your evidence is. It is a simple matter to externally save documents, e-mail, recordings (more on that later in this section), and anything that supports your conclusion.

Third, allow your saboteur to save face. Your peer is someone you will most likely continue to work with in the future. You can deescalate workplace tensions by allowing your co-worker to explain the situation and possibly even apologize if there was a bona fide mistake made. Your objective should be to let your co-worker know that you cannot be walked over and that you are a professional who can handle any situation calmly and firmly.

Fourth, set up a meeting with your manager to apprise them of the situation. If this is something that can affect your career, you need to speak up and identify the problem. Otherwise you only have yourself to blame should something go terminal. You should always calmly and objectively lay out the situation. Once you have reached consensus with your supervisor, it may be appropriate to send out a non-retaliatory e-mail that objectively clarifies the situation and resolution with everyone concerned.

Finally, continue to document the situation with enough evidence to use as validation. Once you believe that you have enough, contact human resources. Set up a meeting with a human resources manager and provide as much information as possible so that they can handle the situation appropriately. Try to distance yourself as much as possible from appearing like a contributor to the problem. Always remain calm and professional.

You might regret the words that come out of your mouth.

"The leader has to be practical and a realist yet must talk the language of the visionary and the idealist."
- Eric Hoffer

Fundamental Rule 3: Loose Lips Sink Ships

When you are trying to impress people with words, the more you say, the more common you appear, and the less in control. Even if you are saying something banal, it will seem original if you make it vague, open-ended, and stoic. Powerful people impress and intimidate by saying less. The more you say, the more likely you are to say something foolish. In my experience, intellectual capacity directly correlates to vocalization. It would appear that loud and aggressive people possess some defect in character and mental capacity. I believe the thoughtful, quiet person may possess finer qualities such as discipline and self-restraint. The silent runner perhaps travels faster and further than another who heralds his or her own arrival.

One of the most difficult lessons I think I've had to learn stems from the things that come out of my mouth. It's not a matter of politically-correct comments or narratives; it is more a case of audience analysis. I've held a long-time belief that I would like to strive to be the person who says less than more. The person who speaks with sage wisdom and not the blathering fool who spews lofty piffle about. There are appropriate times to contribute to a professional conversation. You should not contribute with the driving notion that by not doing so, you appear less of an expert. Quite the contrary is true in actuality and if you are to honestly dissect and examine your own professional conversations, you may find that things are regularly said that do not benefit the situation in some measurable way.

Getting to the point makes the most effective use of everyone's time and resources. You run a significant risk in saying something unnecessary that may haunt you in the future. This self-inflicted mouth wound that you might not even be aware of may negatively impact you. I think of the "butterfly effect as I ponder the possibilities. As I studied my tort law during the first year of law school, I was, on one occasion, focused on duty and breach in negligence, the zone of danger rule discussed, and my mind wandered to things more esoteric, specifically the butterfly effect. The butterfly effect is a phrase that encapsulates the more technical notion of sensitive dependence on initial conditions in chaos theory. Small variations of the initial condition of a dynamical system may produce large variations in the long-term behavior of the system. In law, the Zone of Danger Rule allows a plaintiff to recover for emotional distress or physical harm caused by a defendant's negligent conduct if the plaintiff was in a location where the defendant's conduct could have caused physical harm to the plaintiff. The theory supporting this doctrine is that the likely truth of a claim of emotional distress is increased if the person making the claim came close to suffering physical harm from the conduct that caused the person's emotional distress. The amusing conjunction here is that our actions or deeds, right or wrong, may affect not only those in close proximity, but possibly others located clear across the universe, for better or worse. Getting back to reality here on Earth, the point that am making is that saying only what is relevant and succinct is what is truly appropriate and everything else is superfluous.

I'll offer another example that you will no doubt be faced with in each and every one of your career search activities. Once you are on the market, that is when corporate recruiters start swarming about the "fresh meat" that has become available; this means you, by the way. When you are actively interviewing, keep it to yourself. A recruiter will ask you, "Are you interviewing anywhere else?" or "How long have you been searching for your next position?" And your answer should be "I've only just entered the job search market" or "I am not interviewing anywhere right now," even if you are. Now your ego might try to convince you that you want these recruiters to compete for you. You might want healthy competition for your super special services, but you'd be wrong about that notion. See, the reality is that recruiters are a lot like the opposite end of a potentially romantic relationship. They want to know that you are devoted to them and that there are no other possibilities before them. They are not likely to exude too many resources on you because they know the relationship may not last. Bottom line is this, recruiters don't work for free and they will spend the time and attention to get paid. Why would they take a risk on a candidate that was a flight risk or is not a committed resource? What stops you from wasting their time and resources? Take my advice, keep that nugget to yourself. Your loose lips just might sink your own battleship.

Don't paint a target on yourself willingly

"In matters of style, swim with the current; in matters of principle, stand like a rock." - Thomas Jefferson

Play the perfect executive. The perfect executive thrives in a world where everything revolves around power, precision, and political finesse. You must seem to be a paragon of civility and efficiency. Keep your hands free from both dirt and dirty deeds and you will maintain both your honor as well as positive public perception.

Is there a connection to being on top and not having "blood" on your hands? I might suggest that without it, your underlings might perceive you as weak and antiquated. It may also be that as the puppeteer pulls the strings on his puppets, so too does the effective leader have henchmen to rough things up a bit, all the while remaining pristine.

The more successful you become, the more envy will take root in the minds and actions of those who would do harm to your reputation and success. The more you become exposed, the more you are subject to becoming a high value target. Pay special attention to those around you and be vigilant. Never give anyone the excuse or opportunity they need to disparage or discredit you, especially publically. Never willingly be the victim. You have the power to covertly or overtly neutralize any professional threats to your career. Uneasy lies the head that wears a crown.

Don't tell war stories in an effort to fit in.

War stories tell people something about your ethics, personality. These things follow you into your next battle. An enemy may just decide to clip your wings to protect themselves early on. This takes discipline and patience to achieve positive results. I think the common pitfall is to become too comfortable, too much like a friend to the people you wish to influence. When you do this, you effectively lower your defenses, weaken your position, erode your facade. You cannot grouse, you cannot self-disclose, you cannot reveal too much that is personal or part of some Machiavellian plot lest you snatch defeat from the jaws of victory. Inspiring leaders, however, tell memorable stories. Few business leaders appreciate the power of stories to connect with their audiences.

Stories connect with people on an emotional level. Tell more of them but make sure they don't compromise your power.

Social media

There are many Internet-based social media outlets available to anyone with a rudimentary computer, and the most basic of Internet access service providers have all of the tools necessary to join this Internet evolution revolution. At the time of this writing, I personally have an account on Linkedin.com for my professional public profile needs; a Twitter.com account to broadcast tidbits that entice readers back to some other web site that contains information I would like to share with my global community; a Facebook.com site that really is for surveillance purposes and to keep up with my children or employees. I have maintained a personal blog at MichaelPeters.org for many years and I believe there are many benefits to having it both professionally and personally. I have found that Wiki technology is very useful as well. While I do contribute to many such as Wikipedia.com if I were to be asked by anyone which volunteer activity I am most proud of, it would be my brainchild pet project known globally as the HORSE Project. The Holistic Operational Readiness Security Evaluation (HORSE) project has been a six-year commitment, at the time of this writing, to the education, enlightenment, collaboration, knowledge sharing, and awareness of the global community as it relates to technology law, IT governance, security assessments, awareness and training, governance documentation, compliance, and research. Currently there are hundreds of registered members globally, countless unregistered users, and over 1,600 pages of content present in this collaborative Wiki available to the global community. This has been a true grass-roots effort on my part to raise the bar globally towards how people and organizations approach confidentiality, integrity, and assurances for technological and physical information protections. Interestingly, this project's genesis began with the many years of audit experience in a consultative role with many high-profile clients that appear on the list of Fortune 50, 100, and 500 companies, including Bank of America, First Data Corporation, Humana, and OneOK. The HORSE project eventually evolved into the thesis project for the master's of business administration (MBA) I earned from Western Governors University.

Used properly, portrays the expert whose talents, experience, and credentials are coveted.

Social media is a powerful ally to use when you are riding high and when you are down. The important thing to remember as I have stated many times in this book is to remain consistent. Leaders should never be reactive; they should be proactive. Should you find yourself unemployed, the last thing you need to do is play catch-up with all of the resources at your disposal, resources that you should have been tending all the while.

Social media is a powerful force to be leveraged for our professional and personal benefit. As a leader, even a recovering leader, you should be keenly aware that when solving problems of any kind, the first thing you do is take mental inventory of all the weapons and tools at your disposal. Engage your creativity to find innovative solutions to the problem at hand: your need for a job! I would recommend at almost all costs that you avoid the temptation to latch onto any opportunity that comes your way. Turn down a hundred subordinate positions if you can in order to be positioned for the right executive position. Career continuity is vital to your success and without it, you damage your credibility and viability as a relevant candidate. Appearances matter and using the social media channels to promote a strong personal brand will get you reemployed much faster than passively trolling the job boards waiting for gold nuggets to fall from the sky.

Used improperly, it will get you placed into the unemployment line.

Social media has provided the conduit for any single human to broadcast any message toward a potentially global audience. Within the average twenty-four hour mainstream media cycle, the amateur media cycle occurs exponentially more rapidly. This kinetic potential encompasses the electronic globe in seconds. It has nothing to do with some technical savvy or ability one possesses over the other, but obstacles such as business models, proofing, sourcing, quality control, and audience all govern the flow of electronic news information.

People will not be thwarted in the consumption or dissemination of information. The more tantalizing, the more proliferated the information becomes. For the people who stifle libel, this form of defamation is an emerging and increasing challenge. One only has to turn on any reality show or tabloid on the grocer's shelf to get a distaste for what I'm referring to. These people are generally celebrity status types and don't really equally reflect the average individual or company. It can all be measured by social volume. The more exposed, the more media volume you experience. As a corporate executive leader, you are the celebrity in your industry. You better believe that when I am going to sit down at the table with anyone, I do my homework first. I look for anything related to that person in the search engines and media outlets. I cross reference corporate documents and previous employers.. I've even done background checks on some of the toughest adversaries looking for their weaknesses and skeletons. I fully expect this to happen to me as well and I'd be a fool to act like a fool anywhere on the Internet.

Taking control of the scoop may be the best approach. Sometimes the best defense is a good offense, right? You are either technologically savvy enough alone or enlisting the services of professional spinsters is a prudent course of action. It is virtually impossible to put Pandora back into her box, so why not spin the story your way instead? If opinion and reputation matters, build your case just the same, broadcast your message louder, with authority! Chances are that the deluge created by your own spin cycle will drown out the one created by the opposition. Sometimes you must get a little dirt on your hands to bounce back clean.

I am never surprised, but always intrigued by the apparent need by the larger percentage of the population to disclose, to reveal, to make confessions. So much of this is done to near or complete strangers. Social networks have provided a global forum for confessions (disclosures) to occur. Where once a person who felt so inclined would step into a confessional or spend an hour with a psychiatrist or even Dear Abby, now tweet and text their way to perceived salvation. The fact is that currently 70% of companies reject candidates based on what they find online.

So many facets of our lives are being carried along into public forums. It is becoming more difficult to avoid being recorded by cameras and other audio visual devices. We have grown so accustomed to being recorded that it hardly crosses our minds anymore. The same holds true for our social networks. How much information people reveal is truly astonishing to me. If you believe that the information you reveal electronically is private, guess again. Anything you say, can, and will, be used against you, right?

There is a legal principle I learned in law school known as the The Voluntariness Test, which, in terms of its underlying values, was introduced to evaluate and potentially bar the admission of a confession with doubtful reliability due to the practices used to obtain a confession. Even when reliability is not in question, the question is raised if offensive police practices are used to obtain a confession, or obtained under circumstances in which the defendant's free choice was significantly impaired, even if the police did not resort to offensive practices.

In addition, if adequate Miranda (Recall the "anything you say, can, and will be used against you in a court of law?") warnings are not given prior to a custodial interrogation, incriminating statements made by the accused are ordinarily inadmissible in the prosecution's case in chief. A voluntary confession obtained in violation of an accused rights to adequate Miranda warnings made, however, may be used to impeach him should he testify at trial. In my studies, it is evident that the Miranda Court emphasized that there is no requirement that police stopped a person who enters a police station and states that he wishes to confess to a crime, or a person who calls the police to offer a confession or any other statement he desires to make. Volunteered statements of any kind are not barred by the Fifth Amendment and admissibility is not affected still today. It is very clear that statements not perceived by the Miranda warnings will be admissible when, for example, the defendant walks into a police station and confesses or blurts out an admission when approached by an officer near a crime scene.

This brings me around to my point again. When I investigate computer crimes or identity theft or electronic credit card fraud, I don't limit my hunting and gathering to just the system affected, but I troll the social networks and my business networks looking for associated clues to the perpetrators' identity. Honestly, it is a rare occasion that someone is able to elude being identified and prosecuted. There are so many points of record along the electronic super-highway that dusting all of your tracks is nearly impossible. Your best bet is to get lost in the electronic crowd obscured by the other noise. The "good guys" and "bad guys" use the same tools and tactics. You better believe that I can answer many of those "secret" security questions such as your mother's maiden name because she is one of your Facebook friends and she told me herself, or what high school you graduated from, or that birth date, or even that adorable pet's name. It's all there for harvest time. Say it with roses, say it with mink, say it forever, then say it with hyper-link.

You know what they say about assumptions.

"History is malleable. A new cache of diaries can shed new light, and archeological evidence can challenge our popular assumptions." - Ken Burns

You know who your friends are on moving day, I always say. Or as one of my former associates adjusted my expression to fit the occasion, "You know who your friends are on resignation day." There has rarely been an occasion when I changed employers that some form of unwanted attention was generated from it. I am firmly convinced that my career focus is the catalyst. As a career information security and technology executive, I am required on a routine basis to hire, fire, investigate, remediate, and do whatever it takes to perform my duties. As an enforcer, I am in an unpopular role. There are probably as many jokes made about chief security officers as there are made about lawyers; well maybe we all dislike lawyers more?

When the day comes for you to resign from your executive position and provide a reasonable notice to your employer that is not the time to let your guard down. Do not think for a moment that negative things cannot happen to you. I recall an employer who had a senior IT executive who made it a point of contacting the new employer and throwing that person under the bus, so to speak. He did this to everyone leaving the IT department, apparently. My advice to those employees would be to discuss the matter with the company's general counsel and suggest that a contractual interference and defamation suit may pend in the event that this transpires.

As I have already stated above, you cannot let your guard down during your exit phase of employment. If you are in an enforcer's position, be prepared for negative comments or controversy about you. People seem to like a controversial story so do your best to not give it to them. Better to focus on a smooth transition and remain outwardly subdued about your next adventure. Some of your co-workers will envy your success and do their best to discredit you when you have moved on. You cannot be in an executive position and have tender feelings of a thin skin. Be proud of your accomplishments and continued growth. Share your new status with your social network and the positive spin will drown out the potential negative. I'm not suggesting that this is a transitionary rule because it is certainly not. Just be mindful of the reality that it does occur and be prepared accordingly.

Part 4

Turning adversity into triumph.

"In life, all storms pass, even the figurative ones."
- Michael D. Peters

Fundamental Rule 4: "You never know when you're auditioning."

Occasionally we may find it necessary to regroup. Transitions may be the work that we choose or maybe they are thrust upon us without our permission. I believe that we have an opportunity to use adversity to carve a deeper or alternative path in our careers and in life. We are not required to accept the roles and stereotypes that society assigns us. No, I choose to be the commander of my own life no matter what; so can you do so just as easily. I have the power to reinvent myself if I choose to do so, perhaps one that commands attention. You must be the master of your own image and identity rather than letting the bastards who have knocked you down define it for you. Our modern technological advancements have provided a dramatic conduit in which you can leverage your story. Use these networking and promotional devices we have examined together in previous sections to promote your power, image, and contributions. Doing so will propel you forward, helping shape your future on your terms and not by the wreckage or rhetoric forced on you by others.

With each new change in my life, each new job, home location, or whatever might be considered significant, I look forward to fresh starts. I do try to analyze myself quite regularly, assimilating or enhancing the positive, while eradicating the negative when I identify it. With each change comes an opportunity to be better tomorrow than today.

Have a good cover story: Rehearsed, reasonable, and concise

If you're like most people, you have moments in your life that, given the opportunity, you might have done differently. Some of these occasions may be connected with your personal activities and some are of course connected to professional activities. The bottom line is though, these events have become public in nature and you may either allow the public to arrive at their own conclusions or you may decide to take control of your own story. Interpretations are truly a subjective activity and everyone is certainly entitled to their own opinion. How many times in your life have you heard a rumor or a story about a person that you may or may not have known, and that story turns out to be a complete fabrication, or a mutation of some sort grounded in fact, or the absolute truth? The point I'm trying to make with this is that someone makes a decision to express a situation that has occurred using the language that they understand with an intention for a certain end result to occur. This end result may be completely harmless or utterly malicious. As individuals, the stars of our own show, we are entitled to influence the script.

Potential employers or representatives of some interest you are pursuing will want to explore certain facets of your career history. You should just assume that questions will arise that will require some level of explanation. There is very little that occurs in our own lives that is essentially unscripted, unrehearsed, impromptu, or in some way presents itself in a manner that we are not able to effectively prepare for. Make certain that you will be able to articulate all of the facets of your career history, academic history, or personal social elements that are public to some interested party when the occasion presents itself. Like I said, "you never know when you're auditioning," so it is prudent to be prepared.

    I highly recommend giving some thought to the sequence of events that have shaped your career or personal life and distilling these elements down into simple talking points so that when the need arises, you are prepared to provide a cursory explanation. In the absence of prudent, prior preparation, we have potential chaos. We run the risk of highlighting these potentially inconsistent or undesirable elements in our career or personal history in such a way that they become detrimental to the goals that we are trying to achieve. The chances of successfully passing an examination are diminished without proper, prior preparation right? Why would you then engage in important dialogue with potential employers or sponsors without being properly prepared? I happen to be a very visually-oriented person, and because of this, I'll proceed to mentally role-play with someone I trust in order to practice becoming comfortable with the flow of conversation that is conducive to successfully explaining elements of my career, academic history, or personal life that has become the subject of discussion during an event which I may or may not initiate.

    Perhaps you desire to lead a celebrity lifestyle full of tabloid style controversial articles smearing your good name or revealing some scandalous tidbit of information to the public at large that it is absolutely based in truth. There are consequences that are far-reaching and unforeseen. With the advent of the Internet, inexpensive electronic storage, and most recently, social networking, information potentially will live forever. As our lives become more digitally entrenched, so too do all of the bits, bytes, and pieces.

There has been interesting movements in the courts, particularly in California within the Stored Communications Act space. Specifically, the District Court for the Central District of California, in its Crispin decision, has indicated that content posted to social media personal spaces such as Facebook's "walls," if marked private, could be entitled to protection. The challenge is that even if the Stored Communications Act applies to private messaging and private postings on social media sites, this does not necessarily mean that any and all communications and content shared through social media sites is blocked entirely from discovery by potential litigants or other interested parties such as prospective employers. As you would expect, many social networking sites assert that the Stored Communications Act precludes them from having to comply with subpoenas requesting documents. I recently blogged on the subject, in brief, see **Social Confessions**: http://michaelpeters.org/?p=4897, where I discussed the potential hazards of disclosure within the social networking space. To expound a bit more on the subject, call it **Social Confessions 2**, the bottom line is this: if you're personal information is publicly available on social networking sites, it may be lawfully accessed under the Stored Communications Act. Of course, accessing that information may still be subject to privacy, intellectual property, and other considerations and limitations under U.S. and foreign law, as well as restrictions included in the site's own terms of use, which may be quite complicated itself.

To make matters a bit worse, even if your personal information is not publicly available on a social networking site, the Stored Communications Act still does not preclude "lawful access" to such information. A clever litigant or savvy security professional assisting counsel might take the direct approach and seek the information directly from you or the custodial party under Rule 34 of the Federal Rules of

Civil Procedure, which could help force an unwilling party to provide "lawful consent" to the disclosure of electronic communications held by third parties such as Facebook or MySpace. In a recent decision, see <u>Kathleen Romano v. Steelcase Inc. and Educational & Institutional Cooperative Services Inc.</u>, a New York court ordered a plaintiff in a personal injury case to grant defendant's access to her current and historical Facebook and MySpace pages, even where the information was not publicly available. Relying on such sites' warnings emphasizing that information designated as private may not remain so, the court held that there is no expectation of privacy, no matter what privacy settings were used.

Now a word to the wise. Here is where someone who is technically savvy who really pays dividends to the litigant's attorney or to your spouse's private investigator. When solving a problem or a puzzle, we sometimes need to approach it from different perspectives right? Think about it for a moment, what other avenues might I have to discover content that is posted on private spaces on these social media sites? Even when content that is marked as private on the various social networking services, the same information may be found in person's e-mail in-box, right? Because social media sites frequently send updates to end users through e-mail or text messages regarding other people's postings, comments, and messages, those users' e-mail accounts frequently contain copies of otherwise private social media messages. We suddenly have a much wider attack vector to get the information we desire! I say attack vector deliberately because identity thieves will target your e-mail inbox looking for user names, account names, information, and passwords to steal from you. You should do your best to avoid this potentially compromising situation.

Even if the information sought is not readily accessible, consider whether it can be construed as something other than an "electronic communication." One exception to the Stored Communications Act is the disclosure of "customer records"—that is, "a record or other information pertaining to a subscriber to or customer of such service"—to any person other than a governmental entity. A good example of this would be if your employer wants to know when and how long you were using a particular social media site to defend itself against your wrongful termination suit or if it is building a case against you for a termination event. The dates and times at which an individual accessed a social networking site are not "content" within the meaning of the Stored Communications Act and are therefore not subject to the Stored Communications Act's protections against disclosure. Obviously this is another wide-open attack vector that the technically savvy supporting party to the litigant should be aware of and exploit.

We should certainly expect corporate policies will be updated to make prosecution easier. Laws are evolving and being aware of your rights and how those (intended and unintended) loopholes affect you. Lawyers will continue to need competent and well-credentialed technologists to assist them in pointing out the stones to turn over. Fascinating stuff as far as I am concerned.

I'm honored by your fear

"Fear has its use but cowardice has none."
- Mohandas Gandhi

Everyone has a weakness, a gap in the castle wall. That weakness is usually insecurity, an uncontrollable emotion or need; it can also be a small secret pleasure. Either way, once found, it is a thumbscrew you can turn to your advantage. An expression comes to mind, "A person who lives in a glass house, should never throw stones." Yes of course we could seek every man's vulnerability, but, to what end?

We are with the same activity forcing ourselves into a personal state of elevated readiness. I think it would be difficult to find peace or relax. Another expression, "Loose lips sink ships," comes to mind and is associated with self-destructive behavior if we provide another person to have leverage over us. Pillow talk has brought many a man or woman down for certain.

There have been occasions in my career history, when I discover something within the course of normal duty that relates to the questionable conduct or ethics of a prominent figure. It is absolutely gut-wrenching when it is your direct supervisor. The truth is often avoided because it is ugly and unpleasant. Never appeal to truth and reality unless you are prepared for the anger that comes from disenchantment.

Two situations come to mind when I think about this subject. The first is the public aspect. A person must insert themselves into the public eye if they are to gain any benefits here. A recluse will always remain in the shadows unseen by anyone until they take a risk and step into the light. Nothing ventured, nothing gained. The second facet is the private one. Like marriage or a serious relationship, I think we have a personal duty to inspire and support. Anyone who dwells on the negative is surely doomed to misery. The cold truth about life is that the longer we examine, the more flaws become apparent. As individuals, it is incumbent upon us to perfect ourselves in every possible way. In the process of personal revitalization, we bring springtime into our inner circle. The alternative begins to resemble stale bread.

By default, you are on the losing end of that battle should you decide to act upon the knowledge you have about your supervisor. It would be better to get others to play the cards you are about to deal. The best deceptions are the ones that seem to give the other person a choice: Your opponents feel they are in control, but they are actually your puppets. Give people options that come out in your favor, whichever one they choose. Force them to make choices between the lesser of two evils, both of which serve your purpose.

I think the key revolves around being a strategic thinker. Frequently, we make our opportunities, we seize the moment. It behooves us to understand the big picture and in doing so, we are prepared to identify opportunities that facilitate our goals and objectives. To quote the honorable philosopher and General, Sun Tzu, "He will win who knows when to fight and when not to fight. He will win who knows how to handle both superior and inferior forces. He will win whose army is animated by the same spirit throughout all its ranks. He will win who, prepared himself, waits to take the enemy unprepared. He will win who has military capacity and is not interfered with by the sovereign. If you know the enemy and know yourself, you need not fear the result of a hundred battles. If you know yourself but not the enemy, for every victory gained you will also suffer a defeat. If you know neither the enemy nor yourself, you will succumb in every battle."

I have witnessed situations where a person's insecurity becomes the catalyst for negativity, and reprisal even. When you achieve your goals in business, in academics, in credentials, and achieve success, the possibility is that suddenly you become a perceived threat to someone else who has not invested themselves as much as you have done so yourself. My advice is simple when it comes to mitigating the possibility of being more qualified than the other people in the room, and that is for you to take the quiet road. There is no need to grandstand or bang on the diploma drum anymore. Once you reach the tipping point when you have surpassed the people around you, there is no longer a need to advertise it anymore. Everyone who matters will know and anyone who cannot handle it will forget about it soon enough if it is not persistently in their face.

Credential building

"When one has finished building one's house, one suddenly realizes that in the process one has learned something that one really needed to know in the worst way - before one began." - Friedrich Nietzsche

There is no better time than the present to continue your credential-building efforts. Adding value to your personal portfolio is always a good investment. You should however, make sure that those efforts are conducive to your career progression. To not follow this advice will give others the impression that you are disorganized and attempting to be the subject-matter-expert of subject-matter-experts. You should have already devised your personal career progression project plan and now is not the time to panic, but to stay on the course.

Anything you can do to strengthen yourself as the right candidate, you want to pursue. For example, maybe you have decided that a career in finance is your directional focus, and then perhaps an MBA is what you need to begin working toward. If there is business or regulatory certifications you can secure, do it. Something else that you should not lose sight of either is the power of the network. You should, if you enjoy it, volunteer to contribute to the various organizations out there in the business vertical you have focused on and write blog entries or articles that will showcase you as a subject matter expert and team player. Many of these groups are more than happy to have volunteers moderate the forums and blogs too which is also an avenue to presenting a positive association to your expertise.

There are many other mechanisms for credential building that I have not explored with you. Inspiring leaders bring employees, customers, and colleagues into the process of building the company or service. The command and control way of managing is over. Instead, today's managers solicit input, listen for feedback, and actively incorporate what they hear. This is no less true in social media environments, professional networks, publications, and the corporate space. You never know when you are auditioning.

Flowchart strategy

"Action and reaction, ebb and flow, trial and error, change - this is the rhythm of living. Out of our over-confidence, fear; out of our fear, clearer vision, and fresh hope. And out of hope, progress." - Bruce Barton

As I mentioned in the first part of this book, a particular activity that I have employed for less than a decade and I continue to refine and revise is a very dorky facet of my career preparation activities. The plain reality of this activity is that I have created a simple flowchart representing what I consider to be the Point B, and reverse-engineer the process to the beginning. The way I see it, I can either be an employee, an employer, or a consultant working autonomously. There are very many similar elements to achieve success on the way to Point B. The easiest of the three facets is to be an employee. The reason I say this is because the employer determines what credentials and experience you must have to secure that position. All I have to do is decide what career path I should follow, investigate industry expectations for these positions, and build into my career strategy flowchart these elements as the essential milestone ingredients.

Some of these career-progression flowchart elements are really parallel processes. A great example of what I am referring to would be the book that you are reading now. My primary line of business or career activity is not as an author, but as an executive within the information technology career field for corporate America.

These ancillary activities may potentially become primary activities; however the very fact that I can achieve this independently and in parallel with my primary career does pose some significant benefits. For example, the illustration that follows depicts the decision process I used to secure my first executive position. I researched job boards to find the required and the optional job description requirements and distilled an optimal set of requirements that would represent milestones.

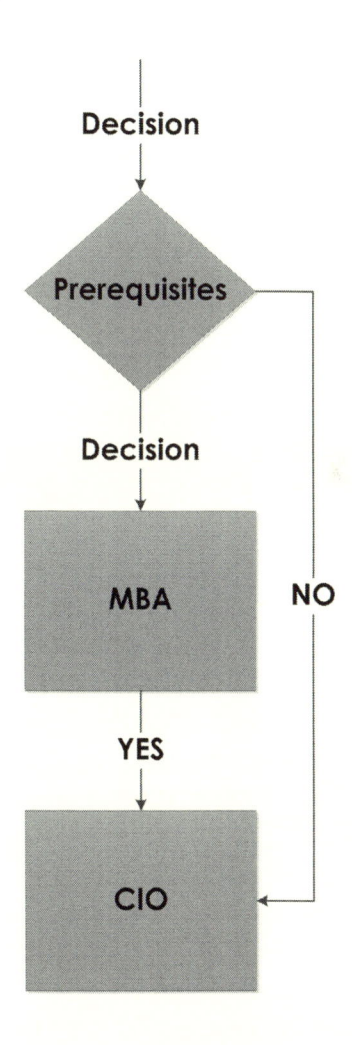

```
            Decision
               │
               ▼
          ◇ Prerequisites ◇─────┐
               │                │
            Decision             │
               │                 │
               ▼                 │
            ┌──────┐        NO   │
            │ MBA  │             │
            └──────┘             │
              YES                │
               │                 │
               ▼                 │
            ┌──────┐             │
            │ CIO  │◄────────────┘
            └──────┘
```

I decided that earning an MBA would be extremely beneficial to my executive career prospects and the fact that that kept showing up in so many executive level job descriptions as an optional requirement just made the business case for me. I recommend always doing more than what is just good enough especially while you have the luxury of time. You never know when you might be in the fight of your career and every edge that you have is one the competition does not.

And this next illustration represents return on investment decisions I needed to make in determining whether my limited time and resources would provide me with a tangible advantage and therefore making that goal worth pursuing.

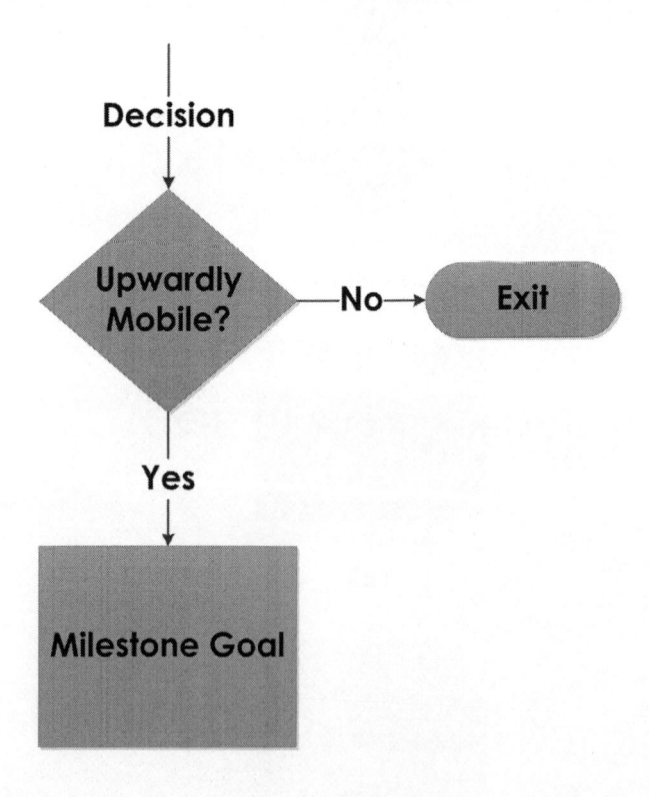

Decision

Upwardly Mobile? —No→ **Exit**

Yes

Milestone Goal

A great example that applied to me was when I was making the decision to pursue or nor pursue a doctorate level degree. Now, this goal far exceeded the normal requirements for most positions I was interested in making application for, but I also am the life learner, remember? Now there was a particular program in decision sciences that I found very appealing and it would dovetail well with my future aspirations, but not very well with my current ones. The only real benefit would have been in the ego department which, generally speaking, will not buy you a cup of coffee. My attention then became fixated on law school. A juris doctorate would be a perfect addition to my executive work as an information security, compliance, legal, and risk management technology officer. How better to surgically take down my criminal opponents? How better to understand how to work with the corporate general counsel or other attorneys?

I was working with a recruited executive on one occasion and when he reviewed my resume, he referred to me as a "weapon" and it made all the hard work worthwhile. Comments like that validate your hard work and diligent attention to your credentials, which is the very heart and soul of getting, keeping, or reclaiming that executive title. Leave nothing to change.

Eyes on the industry

"You can't depend on your eyes when your imagination is out of focus." - Mark Twain

You know the business. You have worked hard along the way to bolster your credentials. You have gained experience, too. Find ways to make your accomplishments seem effortless if possible. Possible employment suitors are everywhere so your actions must seem natural and confident because you are the leader, the optimal candidate. When you act, act effortlessly, as if you could do much more. Present yourself as the accomplished professional. Do your best to avoid the temptation of revealing how hard you have actually worked because it will only draw envy or negativity. Certain decorum must be maintained. This becomes increasingly true the more elevated your position becomes in the circles that you travel. It is certainly prudent to rehearse, to plan, to prepare. These preparatory efforts are a private matter, not a public one. Few people are witness to even dress rehearsal prior to opening night. We must hone our skills and sharpen our blades with as much solitude as might be afforded us. The weakest link in my caper is most certainly the other person.

It is more important, especially when you need a job, to work towards being recognized as the industry's subject-matter expert. Keep up with industry changes, methodologies and mechanisms, and prominent players. Research those leaders you admire the most and consider replicating certain attributes that may have, in part, led to their success. It is always important to remain relevant in our line of work and when we lose site of the future or the emerging leaders in it, we run the risk of becoming an obsolete relic of antiquity.

One of the methods I use to keep my fingertips on the pulse of the industry I've chosen is to keep close contacts with certain agencies and recruiting professionals out there, particularly those who are focused on the executive positions I am interested in. These relationships take time to find and culture of course. For example, I had been attending an industry conference focused on information security and one of the conference speakers was the CEO of a particularly notable industry organization. After some introductory conversations with her and her team in attendance, we found a mutually-beneficial reason to keep in contact. To this day, we maintain our relationship and mutual support. The company's focus is on executive placement within the information security, information technology audit, information technology risk management, and privacy spot every company should have. What a coincidence! I have my eyes on that industry too.

Search agents.

"Joy in looking and comprehending is nature's most beautiful gift." - Albert Einstein

Search agents are your friend. I recommend setting up a personal profile on several career Internet sites even if you are not actively looking for a new opportunity. I look at this activity as keeping in touch with the target market I'm interested in. I will get certain vital bits of information that will make a difference to me when it does indeed come time to seek a career change. First, I will see the available jobs and this will provide me with a sense of the overall market health I'm interested in. Second, I will be able to read firsthand what companies are looking for from a credential and experience standpoint. Knowing that alone will help you shape your personal career-progression project plan. You will see what is expected and be able to adapt your education, credential, and experience focus towards what the market is expecting candidates to have. An observation I made along the way by doing this is that within a ten-year span of time, long enough for the economy to go from good to really bad, organizations debatably required a bachelor's degree and maybe a certification as the low water mark to employment. Now I see master's degrees preferred and specific certifications as the price of admission to secure that C-level position. I fully expect that this trend will continue and within the next ten years, a master's degree will be required along with specific certifications. I recommend being progressive about your credential building because the market continues to demand more and if you don't maintain your credentials, you will begin to miss opportunities and it certainly takes years to acquire many of these crucial academic certifications and experience-based components.

From a holistic standpoint, I've read statistics on recruiting market research, and my friends over at Cornell University suggest that 77% of executive recruiters use search engines to research applicants. What will they find out about you?

Knowledge is power

"An investment in knowledge pays the best interest."
- Benjamin Franklin

The more information you collect, the better decisions you are likely to be able to make. Don't rely on a single source for your information either. Diversified sources of information will get you closer to a realistic impression of your target market. Before you begin your job search campaign again, you must have a personal marketing strategy. A personal marketing strategy provides you with a game plan for your job search campaign.

You should look at the job search as a marketing campaign, with you as the product. Every product, even the best ones, won't succeed without a strong marketing strategy. This begins with a comprehensive, yet flexible plan. First you must know to whom you are marketing. You must identify the types of employers who would be looking for an employee with your qualifications. Are they all within a certain industry? Are there many industries that hire employees with your background?

Salary surveys

"A man's feet should be planted in his country, but his eyes should survey the world."
- George Santayana

Again, it is a great idea to do a little research up front in your chosen area of expertise to ascertain what the going rate is for your talent. In a very short amount searching on the Internet, you will run across many reputable salary survey entities that will assist you in understanding what the normal salary and compensation levels should be expected for your vocation. The most awkward portion of an interview is the discussion of base salary. Enter into this conversation armed with the knowledge of statistical equilibrium.

Special Note: From a compensation standpoint, being an employer gives you the potential to create a compensation structure limited only by the combination of innovation, persistence, and effort applied. As a consultant, there are many variables and as an employee, you are limited to what the prospective employer is willing to pay and what the market limits are for your particular skillset or a traditionally-recognized position.

Don't think that just because you recently came out of a position, especially if you held it for more than five years, that what you think you know what matches with the market rates of today.

Reconnaissance on the competition

"Searching for fossils also comes in many flavors, from microscopic siftings through tiny grains, to overland reconnaissance for suitable bedding settings to uncover bones," - James Garvin

As a career information security practitioner, I have come to learn that everyone has skeletons tucked away in places that are as secret as they are able to make them. Some bigger, some smaller, but they are there nonetheless and depending on how much you want to rectify an injustice or provide yourself with some advantage, you can use this fact for your purposes.

For less than one hundred dollars, you can perform a plethora of background investigations on anyone. If there are criminal records that have not been expunged, you will find them. If they have been expunged, a credit report will reveal the locations for many years where that person lived and you will be able to contact local newspaper companies for an archival search on anything that involves your adversary. Paper publications may be more difficult to search, but they are not dynamic in nature like electronic records can be. Electronic records are much easier to manipulate and delete, however, the very essence of electronic information exists for the ease of replication, transfer, manipulation, and availability. Remember, this applies to you as well. How many times in your life have you witnessed some personality who is in the public eye suddenly become embroiled in scandal or controversy? Those people are fundamentally no different than you or I and we are subject to the same potential pitfalls.

Use at your own risk any information you discover. Discrediting your adversary or creating the same type of damage to them that they caused you might be rewarding emotionally, however, you should be aware that it may open you up to defamation or some other tort lawsuit, should you be discovered. I have been witness to situations where people anonymously reveal disparaging information about their adversary that in the end destroyed their reputation and they lost their job, and I've witnessed people who were unsuccessful in their counter-strike.

There is one thing that is for certain and that is that once disparaging or discrediting information goes public, right or wrong, there is no way to reel in the impression that it leaves with other people, and that effect is lasting. You might lose the initial battle but through human nature, possibly win the war. Private defamation is much harder to validate.

Understand the law

"All ambitions are lawful except those which climb upward on the miseries or credulities of mankind."
- Joseph Conrad

When dealing with adversity, there may be legal remedies to your particular conundrum. Just as when going through life in general, it is beneficial to understand your rights and how the law applies to you. When you are involved with a less-than-desirable work-related situation, the first thing you need to attempt to do is not panic. While this is easier said than done at times, like I've stated many times, look before you leap. Corporations have a process they try to follow that in most cases is predefined and is always crafted or executed to the benefit of the company. Why would you expect anything else?

Employment law is one of the fastest-developing areas of conflict. During the past twenty years, the courts have advanced principles of equal opportunity and fair employment. The delay, costs, and disruption resulting from employment litigation have dramatically diminished the utility of employment litigation for resolving these disputes.

Disputes between a company and its employees can arise in several different contexts. An existing employee may contend that supervisory personnel have harassed them. An employee terminated or denied promotion may contend that such employment action constitutes discrimination based on race, color, religion, sex, national origin, age, or disability. Lastly, a terminated employee may allege that he or she has been wrongfully terminated and that the termination was unfair or without good cause. Federal and state laws reflecting social intolerance for certain workplace conduct, and court decisions interpreting those laws, are redefining the manner in which a company must relate to its employees.

Because of the cost in terms of dollars, morale, and disruption of management, procedures, including mediation, are becoming more common in contracts of employment, personnel manuals, and employee handbooks. In fact, I believe the trend is for the companies to craft sophisticated employment policies that include an elaborate dispute resolution mechanism that may start with an internal complaint and investigation, peer review, non-binding mediation, and then arbitration. All of these will fall under the umbrella of at-will employment, but don't let a company get away with it. One of the greatest weapons you have against a corporation is their reputation. I recall a conversation I had with the general counsel of a firm I worked for concerning a company orchestrated employee termination where dozens of people would have their jobs eliminated. He discussed with me that the corporation anticipated the majority of these people to go away quietly with very little cost to the company. He also mentioned that the company anticipated a small number of people to hire an attorney and threaten litigation which the company was fully prepared to negotiate through mediation as settlement that was much richer than the other folks who went away quietly. You might be interested to know that there were almost no junior or entry-level employees fighting back. The people fighting back were the senior and executive-level employees. The point is, these people were not necessarily smarter or had a better case against the company. They were simply more knowledgeable about their rights and they stood up for themselves. The company feared negative press and negative public perception. Corporate reputation is vital to business success just as reputation is vital to personal success.

Defamation is a legal subject that we should explore briefly since personal and corporate reputations are potentially intimately entwined in it. To be defamatory under the general common law rule, the statement made must hold the plaintiff up to scorn, ridicule, or contempt. The restatement of torts provides that a communication is defamatory if it tends to harm the reputation of another and lower him in the estimation of the community or to deter third persons from associating or dealing with him. A defamatory statement, then, is one that harms reputation by injuring a person's general character or causing personal disgrace. Typically, such communications accuse a person of immoral or criminal conduct. Keep in mind that mere insults, hyperbole, obvious jokes, or pure opinion cannot be the basis for a defamation action. Furthermore, the constitutional interest is highly limited, or possibly absent, in a case involving a private plaintiff in a private matter. It is clear that the First Amendment interests are greatly reduced in the private concern context. It probably should be said that when dealing with legal advice and interpreting the law in your jurisdiction, that seeking out professional assistance is the best course of action.

I have already mentioned earlier that you may decide to fight back by exposing corporate misconduct or exposing your adversaries' dirty laundry in an effort to gain retribution or justice for yourself. Either way, it is not defamation if it is true. The public perception and the corporate perception do maintain negative information, true or false, for a very long time. This reminds me of a personal situation where I was interviewing people for a director level position on my team. A candidate came before me and in looking at his resume, I recognized a company he had been the president for while I was a new customer. His company provided business Internet connections to companies like mine and there were technical troubles with the installation of my services. His company was rather small and he handled many of the communications with customers and technical support. I had noticed deep within an e-mail communication that he had referred to me, his customer, in a derogatory way. Flash forward to the present interview, he initially was thrilled that I knew of him and his company and was confident I would have a happy customer story to regale him with. Much to his chagrin, I revealed my impression of his customer service skills, or the lack thereof and he of course did not get the job. Fifteen years had passed between those moments in time.

To return to my point, it behooves you to understand your rights. Depending on where in the world you live, there are probably laws at the highest levels governing the entire population. Through the various levels of bureaucracy it all trickles down to you. Each layer has subtle differences that all cumulatively affect you and the quality of your life. Understanding the law was one of the catalysts for my decision to attend law school; the others were to more surgically take down my adversaries and to be able to communicate with the lawyers I occasionally interact with.

Contractual rights

"Just give me 25 guys on the last year of their contracts; I'll win a pennant every year." - Sparky Anderson

Have you ever wanted to remember a situation perfectly, to perfectly replay an event in your mind's eye in an attempt to piece together some important scenario? Consider using technology as another tool to accomplish this for you. It is an inexpensive and trivial task now to carry with you a recording device that is discreet and capable of high-quality recordings both for audio and for video. These devices come in all form factors and feature sets now, and it is really amazing. A device that I recently purchased for my own purposes cost me about one-hundred and fifty dollars is capable of twelve hours of recorded audio that is transferrable as a sound file. Just recharge and you are ready to go for the next day.

I will always be an advocate for self-defense and the defense of others. But to discuss self-defense for a moment, you never know when a situation will arise that may boil down to a hearsay event and that recording might mean the difference between losing and proving your point. I have been in situations where I was effectively sucker punched by another person and I was able to use my recording as evidence to neutralize the threat I faced. The softer side of this is certainly in the interest of personal development and being able to positively capture a conversation for completely benign self-enriching reasons. Like they say on the corporate customer support line, "This call may be monitored and or recorded for training and quality control purposes." Two can play that game and in the majority of jurisdictions, you are not required to reveal to the other parties that you are recording.

The question of whether or not to record a phone call or conversation is really a matter of personal preference. Some professionals consider recording an indispensable tool, while others don't like the formality it may impose or introduce during conversations. Some would not consider recording a conversation at all without the other parties' consent, while others do it as a routine course of business.

There are important questions of law that must be addressed first. Both federal and state statutes govern the use of electronic recording equipment. The unlawful use of such equipment can give rise not only to a civil suit by the injured party, but also criminal prosecution. Accordingly, it is critical that professionals know the statutes that apply and what their rights and responsibilities are when recording and disclosing communications.

Wiretapping or eavesdropping is the listening in on conversations of others without their knowledge. Although most of these statutes address wiretapping and eavesdropping, they usually apply to electronic recording of any conversations, including phone calls and in-person communications.

Federal law allows recording of phone calls and other electronic communications with the consent of at least one party to the call. A majority of the states and territories have adopted wiretapping statutes based on the federal law, although most also have extended the law to cover in-person conversations. Today, thirty-eight states and the District of Columbia permit individuals to record conversations to which they are a party without informing the other parties that they are doing so. These laws are referred to as *one-party consent* statutes, and as long as you are a party to the conversation, it is legal for you to record it.

Twelve states today require, under most circumstances, the consent of all parties to a conversation. Those jurisdictions are California, Connecticut, Florida, Illinois, Maryland, Massachusetts, Michigan, Montana, Nevada, New Hampshire, Pennsylvania, and Washington. Be aware that this means that if there are more than two people involved in the conversation, all must consent to the recording activity.

Regardless of the state, it is almost always illegal to record a conversation to which you are not a party, do not have consent to record, and could not naturally overhear from a publicly-accessible location. Federal law and most state laws also make it illegal to disclose the contents of an illegally intercepted call or communication.

At least twenty-four states today have laws restricting certain uses of hidden cameras in private places, although many of the laws are specifically limited to attempts to record nudity. Also, many of the statutes concern unattended hidden cameras, not cameras hidden on a person engaged in a conversation. You should be aware, however, that the audio portion of a video recording will be treated under the regular wiretapping laws in any state. And regardless of whether a state has a criminal law regarding cameras, undercover recording in a private place may prompt civil lawsuits for invasion of privacy by the other party.

By all means, I am making a suggestion that is based upon my experiences and it does not take the place of legal advice from a lawyer in your state. Just as I did and just as you should also, when you are confronted with a legal problem, consult an attorney in your jurisdiction to understand the law and your rights. I am not attempting to address all aspects of electronic recording laws.

Just one other thing to consider while making the decision to play secret agent and record your business day: is there a corporate policy against recording meetings, conversations, and the like? While corporate policy may never overrule the laws of the land, common sense will, however, tell you that you might get terminated for violating corporate policy in doing so. My advice would be that loose lips, sink ships and if you remain discreet, you should be perfectly comfortable with going about recording your business day. I have personally relied on my recording to provide evidence of criminal activity to federal authorities and corporate investigators. Without those recorded events, push comes to shove, and it becomes another hearsay event and your nemesis may very well turn out to be your supervisor; and what a messy jam that turns into. Irrefutable evidence is the objective here. Preserve it well, encrypt it on your computer, index it in a meaningful way, and keep an encrypted backup copy safe offsite until you decide you no longer need that recorded information.

Words of wisdom

"A good head and a good heart are always a formidable combination." - Nelson Mandela

I cannot stress the power of optimism. Inspiring leaders speak of a better future. Extraordinary leaders throughout history have been more optimistic than the average person. The reality is that optimism is a neglected attribute and a powerful weapon in your holistic arsenal.

The trouble with optimism is that it is seen as something abstract and unchangeable. People tend to see themselves as either an optimist or a pessimist, and these two extremes leave no room for any middle ground. I'm guilty at times of classifying myself as an optimist. In reality, we are all optimists by degrees, degrees that are dependent upon changes in external forces and situations. What's more, we all possess the power to alter the way we think, which can lead us to increase our optimism levels.

The times when you need optimism the most is when you are faced with a life problem, a challenge, or some type of setback. If you approach the situation with an optimistic thinking-style during these times, you will increase your resilience, level of hope, and improve your chances of an acceptable or otherwise successful outcome.

The world's pessimists tend to make themselves feel more anxious, depressed, and hopeless, none of which will help them overcome obstacles, deal with tough situations, or persevere with difficult challenges.

Do you prefer to be around more optimistic people or pessimistic people? It is safe to say that the vast majority of people are drawn to positive forces than they are towards negative ones. These people are your employees, supervisors, hiring managers, and significant others.

Like the grand finale of an opera, theatrical performance, or even the performance of an Olympic athlete, planning from start to finish in great detail is integral to success. If you don't know where you are going, then how will you know the way? I have spent an honorable amount of time in the planning of the many facets in life that apply to my interests. Family, career, vocations, even simple projects around the house, have all been planned. I believe that my level of achievement and success dramatically increases with proper planning. A cautionary note is to avoid planning something to the point of a decrease in the desired result. Appropriate planning and then determined aggressive execution is the balance that I strive for. This is a skill that, with commitment, gets better with time. There is a Chinese

Proverb that comes to mind while writing this; "In the struggle between the stone and the water, in time, the water wins." It is a virtue to have patience and it does take time, effort, and dedication to the practice of patience. The plan you devise for yourself is only limited by your own imagination and ambition, nothing more, nothing less my friend.

Closing comments

"To be able to lead others, a man must be willing to go forward alone." - Harry Truman

I hope you have enjoyed this journey as much as I have. Together, we have lifted the veil on what it takes to join the executive ranks and what it takes to remain there on top. The executive leadership road that you have chosen to travel, taking you to the upper corporate echelon, is very challenging, but an eminently rewarding career path. I wish you the very best in this endeavor. It would be great to hear about your success stories and connect with you in the social networking space.

Thank you so much!

Michael

I'm here for you!

Connect with me from within any of the following Internet sites:

- http://michaelpeters.org is the personal blog for Michael D. Peters where discussion topics range from executive leadership, particularly in the technology space, to information security topics, legal analysis, and commentary, participation in Your Personal CISO forum, projects, and the many facets of life learning.

- http://www.lazarusalliance.com/horsewiki/ is the home site for the Holistic Operational Readiness Security Evaluation (HORSE) project Wiki, the brain-child of Michael D. Peters and a very popular Internet resource.

- http://www.facebook.com/Michael.Daniel.Peters is my home page on Facebook.

- http://www.linkedin.com/profile/view?id=6027958&trk=tab_pro is my home on Linkedin and a very good resource for professional relationships, networking with business professionals, and maintaining a great online professional profile.

- http://twitter.com/MichaelDPeters is my less formal side expressed in 140 characters on Twitter. If you are a news and information junkie, Twitter can be a good resource.

- http://feeds.feedburner.com/MichaelPeters Feedburner is a great source for consolidated podcasts and other mobile media.

- http://indeed.com/me/MichaelDPeters Indeed is a great resource to get discovered by recruiters and other professionals alike. Maintain a profile here and you will be amazed at the networking potential that is energized.

- http://technorati.com/MichaelDPeters Technorati was founded to help bloggers succeed by collecting, highlighting, and distributing the global online conversation. Founded as the first blog search engine, Technorati has expanded to a full-service media company providing services to the blogs and social media sites and connecting them with advertisers who want to join the conversation, and whose online properties introduce blog content to millions of consumers. It boasts an audience of over 300 million unique visitors a month worldwide and 150 million people in the US. In July 2010, ComScore ranked Technorati Media as the fourth largest social media property and the third largest blog property.

About the author

Michael D. Peters has been an independent information security consultant, researcher, author, and catalyst with more than twenty-five years of information technology and business leadership experience. In securing his C level, Michael's previous executive positions include Chief Security Officer, Chief Information Security Officer, and advising Chief Information Officer.

Michael holds an Executive Juris Doctorate in Cyberspace Law; a certified MBA in IT Management, BS CIS in IT Security, CISSP, CRISC, CISM, CCE, CMBA, SCSA, and is an ISSA Fellow.

As a highly-accomplished senior IT corporate officer and recognized expert in IT operations, systems, data, and network security, risk and privacy, Michael has already proven his leadership capabilities to many Fortune 50, 100, and 500 companies within the financial, technology, manufacturing, health care, insurance, defense, education, energy, and transportation markets.

Michael is available for speaking, coaching, and consulting by contacting him via his personal blog at http://michaelpeters.org/?page_id=336.

References

Hewlett, Sylvia Ann. (2007). *Off-Ramps and On-Ramps: Keeping Talented Women on the Road to Success.* Harvard Business Review Press.

Maxwell, John. (2007). *The 21 Irrefutable Laws of Leadership: Follow Them and People Will Follow You.* Thomas Nelson Publishing.

Greene, Robert. (1998). *The 48 Laws of Power.* Penguin Books.

King, Donnell. (2000). *Four Principles of Interpersonal Communication.* Pellissippi State Community College.

Knaus, Bill. (2011). *Protect Yourself from Workplace Politics, Stress, and Procrastination.* Psychology Today.

Author's photo by Michael Salem Peters. (2010). MichaelSalemPeters.com.

EFF.org. (2010). *Stored Communications Act,* Electronic Frontier Foundation.

Diamond, Levine, Madden. (2007). *Understanding Torts.* LexisNexis.

University, Cornell. (2011). *Market Your Skills.* Cornell University.

Authenticity, Career. (2011). *Job Search 2.0 Strategies.* CareerAuthenticity.com.

Fox, Nancy. (2011). *The Business Fox.* TheBusinessFox.com.

Miller, Mark. (2011), *Critical Path Partners.* Criticalpathpartners.com.

Cranston, Jane. (2011). *Top 3 Job Search Mistakes Smart People Make.* GreatJobInToughTimes.com.